WITCH HUNT

WITCH HUNT

BOB & GRETCHEN PASSANTINO

*This book is dedicated to the memory of
Dr. Walter Martin, the "Bible Answer Man," and
author of many books including the classic*
Kingdom of the Cults.
*Seventeen years ago he prayed over us and our
ministry before we were even married.
Sixteen years ago he performed our wedding
ceremony.
Since then he has been more than a mentor and a
leader.
He has been a "father in the faith."*

Copyright © 1990 by Bob and Gretchen Passantino

Published in Nashville, Tennessee, by Thomas Nelson, Inc. and distributed in Canada by Lawson Falle, Ltd., Cambridge, Ontario.

Printed in the United States of America.

Unless otherwise noted, Scripture quotations in this publication are from THE NEW KING JAMES VERSION of the Bible. Copyright © 1979, 1980, 1982, Thomas Nelson, Inc., Publishers.

Verses noted NIV are from *The Holy Bible: NEW INTERNATIONAL VERSION.* Copyright © 1978 by the New York International Bible Society. Used by permission of Zondervan Bible Publishers.

Library of Congress Catalog Card Number 89-xxxxx
ISBN 0-8407-3129-9

Printed in the United States of America
3 4 5 6 7—95 94 93 92 91 90

CONTENTS

ACKNOWLEDGMENTS

This book is the product of years of ministry, study, and work with many other Christians. Consequently, our debt of gratitude is owed to more people than space allows us to credit individually. Some gave inspiration, others discipleship, still others pointed out our shortcomings and mistakes. Friends encouraged us, prayed for us, and participated in our work. Thanks to each of them.

Special thanks go to our Answers In Action board of directors: Rick and Cindy Pratt, Bryan and Anne Martin, James Stewart, Joan Moreau, Dan Moen, and Mark Moen. We are also thankful to our church, our pastors and friends there who have been supportive with prayers and encouragement. The late Dr. Walter Martin reinforced for us the importance of using the biblically essential doctrines as our standard in discerning truth from error. Pastor Gene Kirby gave us some of our first lessons in apologetics and taught us that biblical integrity is vital. Jon Schendel and Gary Metz, among their other contributions to this project, encouraged us to begin, impressing on us the need for this book.

Cal Beisner, author and also Gretchen's brother, provided helpful information for Chapter 8 and excellent advice on later drafts of the manuscript. Dr. Norman Geisler acted as a true Christian friend. He carefully reviewed our manuscript, told us where he disagreed, and made suggestions for changes—all of which we considered carefully, and most of which we made. Mark Mittelberg sacrificed time, talents, and treasure to help us polish and edit our manuscript. We are grateful for his insight, logical analysis, and suggestions for restructuring and tightening our arguments.

Finally, Bill Watkins, coauthor of *Worlds Apart* and managing editor of Thomas Nelson Publishers, made this book possible. In addition to his editorial responsibilities, he gave us invaluable help by talking with us through some of the parts of this book and giving positive criticism of our first draft.

FOREWORD

The Late Dr. Walter Martin

It is with great pleasure that I recommend *Witch Hunt*. Bob and Gretchen Passantino have fairly and logically evaluated a thorny problem. In a time when the defense of Christianity has been neglected by many in the Church, they have voiced a legitimate warning.

To unmask heresy is a noble calling, but it should never be used to excuse a personal witch hunt. Some will doubtless attack the authors' motives, but the evidence and logic are irrefutable.

I first met Bob and Gretchen one night seventeen years ago. They were zealous young Christians with a heartfelt commitment to sharing the gospel and defending the faith. I prayed for them that night, asking God's blessings on their earnest desires to serve him. *Witch Hunt* is the latest in a long line of evidence through the years that God did indeed hear my prayer for them. When I began my ministry in 1960, I prayed for God to raise up other dedicated Christians to help fight the battle with me. I am proud to have Bob and Gretchen as fellow-laborers.

This book is well-researched, biblically based, and provides sensible and practical help in the midst of much confusion.

Walter Martin
San Juan Capistrano, California

Nobody Likes A Heretic

Nobody likes a heretic. Everybody wants to be right. But how do you identify the heretics? And who says what's right? Is anybody right all the time?

Several hundred years ago, in a small Massachusetts seaport named Salem, Christians united to vanquish what they perceived to be a major spiritual threat. They were probably motivated, at least in the beginning, by a commendable desire to protect their families, churches, and community from evil. But the methods they used to accomplish their goal resulted in disaster, not freedom from evil. The Salem witch trials are now infamous examples of how the innocent can be accused and condemned unjustly.

Today we have spiritual threats against the church too. Many Christians are committed to ferreting out and banishing heretics—people who appear to be Christians but deceptively introduce corrupt teachings. There is reason to be concerned; the threat is real, just as it was in Jude's day:

> Beloved, while I was very diligent to write to you con-
> cerning our common salvation, I found it necessary to
> write to you exhorting you to contend earnestly for
> the faith which was once for all delivered to the
> saints. For certain men have crept in unnoticed, who
> long ago were marked out for this condemnation, un-
> godly men, who turn the grace of our God into licen-
> tiousness and deny the only Lord God and our Lord
> Jesus Christ (Jude 3–4).

Response to this threat is growing, and Christians
everywhere are becoming alert to spot and expose
heresy. But good motives alone do not ensure a successful "hunt." Due to faulty methods and techniques (what we call "witch hunting") many people—
including brothers and sisters in Christ—have been
hurt.

DEALING WITH UNAVOIDABLE CONTROVERSIES

The weapon of scriptural discernment is very
powerful and in the right hands does an excellent job
of defending doctrinal integrity without inadvertently wounding innocent Christians. But that same
weapon in the wrong hands too often attacks indiscriminately—wounding the innocent as well as the
guilty and even sometimes aiming so wide of the
mark as to let some of the guilty escape intact.

We have watched an alarming trend develop over
the last seventeen years of our ministry. What
started as scattered problems resulting from a few
well-meaning, zealous but ill-equipped Christian
"discerners," has grown into a new evangelical industry—witch hunting.

Most people involved in the ministry of defending
the Christian faith (referred to as *apologetics,* a term

derived from the Greek word *apologia,* translated "defense," in 1 Peter 3:15) have noble goals: to preserve Christian doctrine and the Church from contamination by the world and Satan, and to advance the cause of the gospel against unbelief. But sometimes even the best of us use weapons wrongly and against the wrong targets. Perhaps our zeal outstrips our maturity: we don't have the proper background, training, experience, or sometimes we even misunderstand biblical and practical Christianity. This can cripple us, handicapping us from being able to tell the real heretic from the merely ignorant or even from the orthodox Christians who do not look or sound just the way we *think* all Christians should look and sound. But regardless of the reason or the motive, the consequence is the same—someone is mislabeled, misunderstood, and often left with an undeserved wound. A fellow believer and his ministry are hurt, sometimes permanently. We believe it is a tragedy that can and should be avoided.

OUR CONCERN

Some readers may suspect that this book is motivated by special interests, pressure, financial lures, or even hidden ties to those who have been targets of witch hunting.

That is not the case. In the years we have been involved in counter-cult ministry, we have cooperated with many different cult-watching organizations, including Christian Research Institute (where Gretchen worked as Senior Research Consultant for six years), Spiritual Counterfeits Project, *Cornerstone,* and many others. We directed Christian Apologetics: Research and Information Service (CARIS) for years before founding Answers In Action. CARIS was especially known for work in evangelizing Jehovah's Witnesses and organizing witnessing teams in response to various cultic events. We are authors of *Answers to the Cultist at Your Door,* which won the Gold Medallion Award for Christian Education, one of the premier awards in Christian publishing.

Through Answers In Action we are attempting to broaden the influence of Christians by helping them impact every area of their lives with the strength of biblical teaching. Answers In Action is a nonprofit religious organization, supported by donations from the general public and not dependent on any other organization or individual. Our board of directors includes Christians from a number of different churches.

OUR MOTIVATION

Our motivation is the same as that of researcher Georgie Kinyon (of We Care Ministries) who observed firsthand some of the extremes of witch hunting:

Within the last few years many Christians are seeing errors coming into the Charismatic and Pentecostal movements and are acting out of a sense of fear. As we both are aware there are grave problems within the Christian world right now. It seems as if there are sides Christians are joining. Ones behind the Dave Hunt and Hal Lindsey camp, the others behind the Apologist camps, and others behind the Evangelical camps. Each aiming arrows at the others and not reasoning out what is happening within our world, and perhaps laying aside our differences on eschatology long enough to examine the real issues at stake. . . .

Instead what I have found (consistently), because of the many divisions within the camps, no one desires to examine the others' position and maybe lay aside their differences long enough to reach out to those who are dying and crying within our Christian churches. ... I am afraid of seeing those whom are covered by our King's blood becoming even more deceived, and we who have the answers are fighting among ourselves.[1]

WHAT THIS BOOK IS

Perhaps you have been concerned about the subtle deceptions the Enemy has practiced on Christians, especially in the Church. You want to be able to identify those deceptions, vanquish them with the power of God's Word, and protect yourself from false belief or practice. But you are concerned that some of the "discernment" information you have been hearing or reading about is not quite adequate. This book will help you identify witch hunting; compare it to biblical discernment patterns; and offer positive and constructive biblical principles which can be used to protect the integrity of Christ's Church, while you effectively defend the faith and share the good news to those without faith.

There is a lot of specific documentation in this book. We have not been timid about identifying witch hunting, even when it has been practiced by us, our colleagues and friends, or other popular Christian teachers and authors. We would never cast doubt on the sincere and deep commitment to Jesus Christ of those cited, nor on the biblical basis for their ministries. We realize that we walk a fine line between necessary, constructive criticism and what could become our own brand of witch hunting. But our purpose and goal is to improve the Christian's defense mechanisms, not sabotage them. We cannot agree with either witch hunting or its consequences, and this book not only presents the scriptural justification for our disagreement; it also gives a concise biblical guide for accurate discernment.

We are bound to receive criticism no matter what we say in the pages that follow. If we defend a particular witch hunting target, some readers are likely to assume wrongly that we therefore believe the target must be completely orthodox. If we defend ten witch hunting targets and do not mention ten others, some readers will assume that the unmentioned ones therefore must be heretics.

And we will probably be accused both of "letting the guilty go free on a technicality" and conversely, of "exposing" the innocent to more controversial publicity. But two of the core witch hunting problems we find are: (1) often the innocent as well as the guilty are caught by witch hunting tactics; and (2) the guilty are often caught by the wrong methods, thus allowing them an "out." Because of our commitment to biblical discernment, we cannot avoid this controversy, and we ask you to understand this book in the spirit in which it is written.

This book is designed to *show how witch hunting techniques unfairly condemn people and ministries*. Does this mean that each person and ministry mentioned here is actually orthodox and innocent of all error? *Not at all*. It simply means that the *technique* used to judge orthodoxy and innocence is either the wrong technique or is used wrongly.

For instance, because both the Jehovah's Witnesses' organization and Mormonism deny the cardinal biblical doctrines (the Trinty, etc.) and yet claim to be Christian, both are cults. However, it would be *unfair* to accuse Jehovah's Witnesses of thinking they can become gods. It would also be *unfair* to accuse Mormons of thinking that the Holy

Spirit is not a person and is not God. *Becoming gods is a Mormon belief*, and *denying the deity and personality of the Holy Spirit is a Jehovah's Witness belief.* Understand this: both Mormonism and Jehovah's Witnesses are cultic, heretical, unbiblical, and non-Christian. However, *we cannot honestly and fairly claim to represent the God of truth—the God whom we claim to serve—by accusing anyone unfairly.*

It is vital to remember that our criticism of witch hunting techniques is not necessarily an endorsement of the victims of witch hunting.

WHAT THIS BOOK IS NOT

This book is not designed to evaluate the New Age Movement, the extent of New Age incursion into the Church, or the actual orthodoxy or heterodoxy of persons and organizations criticized by those engaged in witch hunting. It is *not* a book on heresy in the Church. It is *not* a book criticizing the Prosperity Movement, healing in the atonement teachings, several varieties of secular psychology, "name-it-and-claim-it" trends, compromising of Christian truth, aberrant practices in the Church, immorality among televangelists, or many other evils in the Church *with which we have serious theological disagreement.* One book cannot do everything. You can consult the "For Further Reading" section for books which deal with these matters.

There are many Christians, including many counter-cult experts, who agree with us that a number of people and organizations have been criticized unfairly by witch hunting techniques. However, nobody can really know who is deliberately wielding witch hunting weapons and who is inadvertently doing so, while believing he or she is doing the very best job possible to discern truth from error (1 Thess. 5:21–22). We do not pretend to know who is deceitful and who is honest. That is not our task as Christian discerners. Romans 14:10–13, speaking of different opinions concerning food, drink, and ritual, provides a cogent parallel:

> But why do you judge your brother? Or why do you show contempt for your brother? For we shall all stand before the judgment seat of Christ. For it is written: "As I live, says the LORD, every knee shall bow to Me, and every tongue shall confess to God." So then each of us shall give account of himself to God. Therefore let us not judge one another anymore, but rather resolve this, not to put a stumbling block or a cause to fall in our brother's way.

OUR OBLIGATION

Our discernment obligation is to distinguish truth from error, orthodoxy from heresy, right from wrong. But our obligation is *not* to judge the motives or intentions of any of those we mention as using witch hunting techniques. Were we to keep silent, we would fail to fulfill our discernment obligation. Were we to judge the motives of those engaged in witch hunting, we would also become guilty of witch hunting.

Counter-cult researcher Eric Pement, assistant editor of *Cornerstone* magazine, said,

> I have come to think of cult researchers as being like scouts, who work for a while in Enemy territory, studying the Enemy's tactics and literature, who then come back to the army in the field to warn them of dangerous areas. Many cult researchers have dif-

ferent areas they specialize in, but they're all on the
same side, working under the same Commander, and
sharing and cross-checking their information with
each other.

If one of us should get some misinformation, then
may the Lord enable us to receive correction from the
others or from the Lord's Word, and then to get back
to the business at hand, to the work God has called us
to. We are called, in a way, almost to a double duty: to
evangelize the lost, those in the Enemy's camp, and to
strengthen the Church, to warn of dangers ahead,
and to train those in the Church to evangelize cultists
effectively.[2]

Our fervent prayer is that proper biblical discernment will overcome where witch hunting has been
the norm, and that consequently Christians will be
challenged to spiritual excellence and nonbelievers
to repentance.

If you have ever wondered how to tell the good
from the bad in today's contemporary religious
smorgasbord of ideas, beliefs, and practices, you can
find out how in this book. We cannot depend on
witch hunting, but we *can* depend on biblical discernment

Bob and Gretchen Passantino
Costa Mesa, California
January, 1990

CHAPTER 1

Tragedies of the Hunt

CIVILIAN CASUALTY

*T*he voice of the woman on the phone trembled as she tried to explain why she needed so desperately to see us right away.

"You don't understand. I'm in real spiritual danger! I might be demon possessed already! Can't you help me?"

Andrea had been a Christian for six years, had a strong and supportive Christian husband, and was active in her church. But she found it impossible to maintain a normal relationship with her alcoholic parents, especially with her stepfather, who had sexually abused her for more than eight years until she left home at seventeen to marry. Her husband urged her to see their pastor for counseling. She learned how to apply scriptural principles to her feelings and her relationship with her parents. She began to trust God more.

Then a friend gave Andrea a copy of a popular book which purported to expose the occultic, New Age foundation of all modern psychology. The friend warned Andrea, "Pastor Joe has a degree in psychology. All that psychology stuff comes from Jung, who was an occultist, and Freud, who was an atheist and a sexual pervert. You may think you're being helped, but you're really buying into occultic heresy."

Andrea read the book. She confronted Pastor Joe. He responded that he was doing his best to counsel her from the Scriptures and that his psychology background merely gave him a few tools and perspectives to help him relate the Scriptures specifically to her problems.

Andrea reread the book. She could not see any way out of it. She had compromised her faith and participated in witchcraft. She probably had a deceiving spirit or demon that was tricking her into thinking her problems were being solved in a biblical way.

By the time Andrea saw us, she was fearful that she had opened herself up to demonic invasion. She and her family had not attended church for six weeks because they could not agree on where to go. Andrea's frustration showed as she finished, "I guess everyone can have a good laugh on me! I try to get myself straightened out and end up demonized!"

BATTLE CASUALTY

John had only been a Christian for three months when he heard a well-known speaker in his church talk about the false beliefs of Jehovah's Witnesses. Inspired by the speaker's story of deliverance from fifteen years as a Jehovah's Witness, John began sharing the gospel with Jehovah's Witnesses. Pretty soon he was spending every evening witnessing and weekends sharing his message in local churches. He was so busy that he didn't have much time to study, and theological and doctrinal issues were too deep for him to grasp quickly. So he picked up what he felt were the quickest and easiest ways to show Jehovah's Witnesses that they were wrong. He figured that once he proved to them that the Watchtower had lied to them, they would accept the gospel easily. It seemed an easy, practical solution which enabled him to promote the gospel without really having to acquire an in-depth understanding of basic biblical doctrine.

Then John started discussions with two leading Jehovah's Witnesses. He kept pressing home to them that the Watchtower organization was a false prophet. They kept pressing home to him that it was irrational to believe in the Trinity and that he couldn't answer their scriptural arguments against the deity of Christ. Every time he brought up organizational flaws, they brought up arguments against the deity of Christ. At first John didn't pay much attention to what they said. After all, he reasoned, other Christians seemed to understand and be able to defend the doctrine of the Trinity, and he thought that if he could just discredit the Watchtower, they would drop this stuff about Jesus being created.

But that did not happen. The Jehovah's Witnesses finally got to him by convincing him that even if the Watchtower was flawed, at least they worshiped only one God and did not commit blasphemy by making Jesus God when he was only an angel. Eventually John was baptized a Jehovah's Witness and began going door to door sharing the "good news of the kingdom" from *The Watchtower* and *Awake!* magazines.

His "quick answers" weren't enough to protect him from the seduction of heresy.

SNIPER CASUALTY

Jeff was a public school teacher and a Christian. Over the years he had learned how to use the public school system and its myriad rules and regulations to get the fairest treatment possible for Christian students and teachers and their activities. He spearheaded a drive to get Christian clubs approved on local high school campuses. He coordinated parents' legal moves to get district approval for the inclusion of "Silent Night" and "Joy to the World" in the district winter concert.

Jeff learned a lot from other Christian education organizations and worked closely with national Christian parents' and Christian teachers' organizations. His church asked him to lead a study group for parents on how to protect their children's faith in the public school system. Soon other churches and Christian organizations had him lead study groups for them. The demand out-paced his time, so he trained other teachers and parents to lead even more study groups. He was especially gratified when the largest evangelical church in the city asked him to lead study groups for them.

Then one day Jeff got a call. The pastor of the large church was canceling his study groups immediately. A member had come to him with confidential (but unsubstantiated) information that Jeff had obtained funds to print his study group workbooks from the local Catholic church. In addition, the member had heard that Jeff believed in infant baptism instead of believer baptism only. So the pastor had decided, without reading the workbooks, that Jeff's study groups were probably contrary to his church's doctrine too.

Jeff tried to talk with the pastor and resolve the

problems, but he was unavailable. After all, he had to administer a several-thousand-member church. He did not have time for fruitless discussions. Besides, he probably reasoned, God would likely give Jeff a better opportunity elsewhere. Jeff should just look at it as a blessing in disguise.

WARFARE IS DANGEROUS

The people in these stories are battle casualties of witch hunting. Each of them had a heart for doing God's will, and each of them was sabotaged by witch hunting. The Bible tells us to defend orthodoxy (Jude 3), to check our faith (1 Thess. 5:21–22) and to fight Satan and his influence (Eph. 6:10–17). But we must be sure that we are mature, knowledgeable, and led by the Spirit to discern properly.

Some discerners, lacking a comprehensive and lucid understanding of essential biblical doctrine, tend to condemn anything they are not familiar with, assuming that it is better to condemn than risk letting even one heretical belief slip in. Other discerners take the same lack and do not condemn anything, assuming that "unity" is necessary at all costs, even if the one they "feel" is a believer actually espouses heretical doctrine.

Christians should not be satisfied with either of these forms of slipshod discernment. Those who wrongly attack true believers, even unwittingly, imitate the godless who "with his mouth destroys his neighbor" (Prov. 11:9). Those who compromise essential Christian belief in the name of unity, even though they are sincere, often embrace evil (1 Thess. 5:22).

UNAVOIDABLE CONTROVERSIES

Most of us try to avoid controversy as much as possible. We want people to like us; we desire to fit in; we do not wish to rock the boat. But as Christians we have strong convictions, and there are times when we cannot stay out of controversy without compromising our Christian sense of right and wrong.

Throughout the history of Christianity, there have been Christians who have jumped into the middle of controversy because they were compelled by their ultimate biblical values. The apostle Paul could have ignored the pagan idols in Athens and concentrated on bringing the gospel to the Jews there. Instead, Scripture tells us, "His spirit was provoked within him when he saw that the city was given over to idols. Therefore he reasoned in the synagogue with the Jews and with the Gentile worshipers, and in the marketplace daily with those who happened to be there" (Acts 17:16–17).

When a fourth-century bishop, Arius of Alexandria, denied the deity of Christ and asserted that he was not eternal but was created by the Father, orthodox church leaders could not remain silent. Though the controversy raged for decades, and some leaders suffered exile and persecution for their outspoken defense of the deity of Christ, the fight was worth it. The chief defender of orthodoxy in this debate, Athanasius, was once admonished, "Athanasius, the world is against you." Athanasius' reply epitomizes the courage of biblical conviction: "No, Athanasius is against the world!"

WHEN THE CONTROVERSIES
BECOME COMPLEX

But controversies are not always so clear-cut. At times it's hard to tell the good guys from the bad. Sometimes even the principal players cannot articulate their own views, much less argue clearly against the opposition. Very rarely do Christians disagree about issues that are black and white. For example, all Christians agree that anyone who denies Jesus Christ cannot be of God. And we do not have a problem speaking out against immorality, dishonesty, or terrorism.

But often the issues are complex. It is not always easy to make clear-cut judgments or to recognize instantly the best biblical reaction.

Most Christians agree that abortion is not a Christian option: killing an unborn child is just as immoral as killing a born child. But what is the "Christian response" to a woman who has had an abortion under extreme pressure and while believing the pro-abortion claim that she is just excising a piece of tissue from her own body? Do we ostracize her for her sin? Do we ignore her and hope she doesn't bring the subject up? Or do we extend the love and forgiving grace of the Lord to her and risk miscommunicating approval for what she did?

And how far should our opposition to abortion go? Should all Christians take an active part in opposing abortion? Is putting a pro-life bumper sticker on your car enough? Or should you be picketing? And if you really believe abortion is murder, then can you justify breaking the law, perhaps by peacefully and passively blocking access to an abortion clinic to oppose abortion? These questions are not easy to answer.

Most Christians agree that one's gifts to the Lord's work are a private matter and that we should not brag about the contributions we make to our church or other Christian ministries. But is it acceptable for a Christian to declare his charitable contributions on his income tax form so he can pay less in taxes and thereby have more to give to the Lord? Is that a mingling of his commitment to support the Lord's work with a desire to increase his own wealth or to record his great generosity?

Most Christians agree that unprovoked aggression is completely unethical and immoral. Many Christians believe that self-defense (or defense of one's family, community, or nation) is the only justification for any use of force. Other Christians believe that absolute pacifism is the only Christian option. Christians holding each of these views have little problem describing their positions in light of simple hypothetical examples. But life is often more complex than hypothetical examples. The United States bombed Libya three years ago in an apparently successful attempt to dissuade that terrorist nation from any further direct acts of terrorism on American citizens traveling abroad. But the United States' bombing also killed some innocent persons, including one of Mohamar Khaddafi's young children. Was the United States' action unprovoked aggression, murder, or self-defense? Can a Christian who believes only in self-defense work in a bomb factory? What about a factory that only makes test equipment for military vehicles and is not engaged directly in making weapons? How would an absolute pacifist reconcile personal responsibility when his refusal to intervene with physical force (perhaps not even deadly force) allows a terrorist to torture and murder innocent victims?

Witch hunting proliferates when sincere but ill-equipped Christians jump into the middle of unavoidable complex controversies and combine faulty techniques and rash judgments with complex issues. There is nothing wrong with questioning, exploring new ideas, or trying out theories to see whether or not they are valid within the process of searching for truth and certainty—even when we make mistakes. In fact, learning from our mistakes is invaluable. But when we fail to exercise proper discernment, when we substitute exploration for discovery, then we fall into witch hunting. Witch hunting occurs when Christians, desiring to preserve truth, do not finish their work carefully and instead (1) misunderstand or misuse Scripture; (2) argue illogically; (3) misrepresent others; or (4) by their actions assume that the end (preserving truth) justifies the means (unfair accusations).

BACKGROUND TO CONTEMPORARY
WITCH HUNTING

Several years ago we noticed a growing trend in Christian apologetic, or discernment, organizations. Many Christians, realizing the rising threat of the cults and the occult in the late 1960s and 1970s, eagerly committed themselves to learning apologetics and actively evangelizing cultists. That zeal and compassion was commendable. However, as happens often in quickly growing movements, many of these Christians failed to spend the necessary time to study and develop well-rounded, sound apologetic approaches. There was not enough teaching or support on the local church level to provide adequate training for new cult apologists. The problem was compounded immeasurably when lay Christians be-

27

gan copying these well-meaning but ill-equipped apologists.

The blame for much of the witch hunting we see today can be laid squarely on the shoulders of the American Christian churches. American Christians were ill-equipped to confront the claims of the cults because for too many years churches bought the secular lie that Christianity has no part in the world and should confine itself to its own private cloister. Threats of theological liberalism, scientism, agnosticism, and immorality caused many churches to isolate themselves from the world and its problems, wrongly telling themselves that Christians should only preach the gospel—or risk "compromising with the world." The cults flourished as the churches retreated from public engagement. Cultic doctrine flourished as Christians became unable to explain their beliefs in any terms but their own in-group vocabulary.

When Christians woke up to the threat of the cults, they had very few seminary or Bible school courses, or theological books, which dealt clearly and expressly from a biblical basis with cultic doctrine and cult apologetics. If a Christian wanted to learn the right way to evangelize cultists, where could he go?

And so these people began teaching themselves. They began sharing the gospel and defending the faith at the same time they were trying to plow through thick theology books and "translate" Christian vocabulary so that cultists could understand what they meant.

The quality of the few available materials was uneven. Charles Braden had a general knowledge of world religions and deviations from normative Christianity; Dr. Marcus Bach presented a liberal perspective on the cults; Anthony Hoekema gave a conservative commentary on a few of the major cults; Harvey Cox became the media funnel for many cults; and Walter Martin provided a popular conservative biblical response to the cults. But in spite of the teaching examples of evangelicals such as Walter Martin and Anthony Hoekema, the competition was sparse enough that ill-equipped people rose to positions of leadership.

LEARNING THROUGH EXPERIENCE

We will never forget how God taught us the insufficiency of our biblical preparation when we were new to cult apologetics. We had a close friend who had fallen away from the Lord. We had not seen him for almost a year, and we finally cornered him after his swing shift at work. He agreed to go with us to an all-night coffee shop to talk about the Lord. But we were so enthused about our ministry to the cults that we spent all night in the coffee shop talking to him about how to prove the deity of Christ to a Jehovah's Witness. We never once talked about his estrangement from the Lord or the biblical steps to repentance.

Later God convicted us for our insensitivity: We knew many arguments for the deity of Christ, but we lacked the theological depth and maturity to share openly with our friend about his own walk with the Lord. We had learned how to witness to cultists without learning to incorporate the full counsel of God's Word into our lives. We were great at pointing out heresy, but lacked sensitivity to other Christians who had spiritual problems. Our friend had orthodox doctrine; he believed the right things. But he lacked a dynamic and intimate walk with the Lord. We did not recognize our responsibility as his Christian friends to admonish and encourage him to go to the Lord with his needs. The Lord taught us from this experience that we should learn proper doctrine and practice from those who were strong in those areas. We realized that doctrine without sensitivity is heartless, and compassion without truth becomes compromise.

WHERE CAN WE FIND WITCH HUNTING?

This is the dilemma into which many of us unwittingly fall: we draw doctrinal dividing lines without discerning the relative importance of different doctrines, and we often assume that compassion equals compromise.

Often we know what is heretical, but we do not know how to show it logically or biblically. Witch hunting techniques do not provide clear biblical standards for discerning truth from error, believer from nonbeliever. And they often result in a tendency to condemn everyone out of hand, perhaps with the thought, "Better safe than sorry."

Probably all of us who participate in biblical discernment have a few areas where we slip unwittingly into witch hunting. Even if we inadvertently use a wrong technique in this book, it does not negate the rest of the points we make. And even those who seem to make a habit of witch hunting sometimes are accurate and discerning. But being right accidentally or infrequently is no excuse for misusing leadership positions or Scripture interpretations.

BIBLICAL DISCERNMENT

Biblical discernment involves an understanding of both good and evil. In 1 Kings 3:9, Solomon described biblical discernment in his prayer to the Lord as "an understanding heart to judge Your people, that I may discern between good and evil."

That is a simple description, but it contains some complex truths. It implies a biblical compassion and love that desires for one to be reconciled to God and growing in his truth. An understanding heart also encompasses the ability to bring the truth to bear in love, not shirking accountability but not withholding compassion either. The golden rule can be applied to apologetics too: Any tool or Scripture I use to confront you, I should be able to face also.

This passage assumes that it is sometimes proper to judge. Many people, Christians and non-Christians, repeat the phrase, "judge not . . . ," from Matthew 7:1 but ignore its context, which validates judgment as long as that judgment is equitably distributed over the critic and the criticized: "Judge not, that you be not judged. For with what judgment you judge, you will be judged; and with the same measure you use, it will be measured back to you" (Matt. 7:1–2). Both the Matthew and the 1 Kings passages endorse judgment which uses God's revelation as its standard but warn against prejudicial or relativistic judgment. In John 7:24 Jesus tells us, "Do not judge according to appearance, but judge with righteous judgment." And Paul tells us, "He who is spiritual judges all things" (1 Cor. 2:15). The Bereans gave us a good example of biblical judgment. They checked everything the apostle Paul taught them, using the Scriptures as their standard (Acts 17:11).

Biblical discernment is absolutely necessary for Christians living in a world of many ideas, beliefs, and practices. Without a clear understanding of biblical truth (2 Tim. 2:15) and accurate discernment between good and evil (Prov. 2:1–11), Christians are unable to enjoy free fellowship with other believers and confidence in the face of opposition. Without biblical discernment, Christians end up living in fear and confusion, unable to walk confidently in truth and love. The result of using godly wisdom is described by Solomon:

> Keep sound wisdom and discretion;
> So they will be life to your soul
> And grace to your neck.
> Then you will walk safely in your way,
> And your foot will not stumble.
> When you lie down, you will not be afraid;
> Yes, you will lie down and your sleep will be
> sweet.
> Do not be afraid of sudden terror,
> Nor of trouble from the wicked when it comes;
> For the LORD will be your confidence,
> And will keep your foot from being caught
> (Prov. 3:21–26).

INADEQUATE DISCERNMENT MISSES THE MARK

Again, anyone, from simple young believers to professional theologians, can slip into discernment techniques which do not deal fully and biblically with complex controversies. It is easy to slip from mature defense of the faith into unthinking witch hunting even though we are sincere Christians who love God and believe that we have an obligation to protect the Church from harm.

Why do Christians sometimes label as heresy anything with which they are unfamiliar, even when there is no clear-cut and deliberate doctrinal deviation evident? The answer to this question is directly related to common lacks in preparation for and execution of biblical discernment.

Lack of Theology

Witch hunting is characterized by a lack of evident theological education or study. Many Christians who are former cultists or occultists, for example, are thrust into leadership and teaching positions shortly after their conversions, before they are able to obtain sound theological teaching from their own pastors, other Christian leaders, or in a formal Bible school or seminary. Regardless of background, a lack of theological preparation often evidences itself in the witch hunting tendency to label as heresy anything which is unfamiliar.

Here's an example we often encounter since we speak in so many different kinds of churches. People from churches that have informal worship services and spontaneous prayer sometimes complain to us, "I know why traditional churches are so boring. They write out all their prayers and follow the same order of service every week. No wonder the Spirit's not there!" But then from people who attend churches that formalize their worship services and have prayers written in their bulletins, we sometimes hear, "Nontraditional churches show no respect for God. Everything happens by accident. Why don't they care enough about worshiping the Lord to spend time planning what would be edifying to him? And who can get inspired by a spontaneous prayer when every other word is 'just' or 'um'?" Witch hunting confuses different with wrong.

Lack of Professional Association

Sometimes Christians are so caught up in their dedication to spending every moment teaching and defending the gospel that they develop little or no working relationship with other cult researchers or apologetic organizations. Although there is nothing sacrosanct about established ministries, the Bible does present the general principle that the younger should learn from the older, the less experienced from the more mature (1 Thess. 2:10–12). One of the ways God has given us to check our own faith and our own understanding is to learn from other mature believers who have already gone through what we are just learning.

Here's an example from a fine Christian apologist we respect. Dr. Norman Geisler is not only a well-respected philosopher, author, and professor at Liberty University, he is also strongly opposed to abortion. He has dedicated a significant portion of his time to speaking out against abortion, picketing abortion clinics, teaching his students to oppose abortion, and supporting the pro-life community. He strongly believes that abortion is wrong and that unborn children are just as valuable and human as any other children.

However, when Dr. Geisler first wrote his book *Ethics: Alternatives and Issues* in 1971, two years before Roe vs. Wade, very few Christian theologians or philosophers had comprehensively studied or written on the subject of abortion. In fact, most of the religious commentary on abortion was from liberal theologians who argued *in favor* of abortion. Geisler took a strong stand against abortion and was one of the first conservative Christians to deal seriously with the issue. However, he wrote, "Abortion is not necessarily murder. . . . [An unborn baby] is a being with an ever increasing value as it develops," and "a human embryo is a *potentially* human being. . . ." (italics added)[1]

Today Dr. Geisler has changed those lines and affirms that his thinking on the subject has deepened and become more biblically sound. He knows for sure that every unborn child is just as human and just as valuable as any other human being. Over lunch one day he told us, "At the time I was one of the most conservative voices on the issue. But there weren't enough of us who had done enough thinking and discussing to cover all of the intricacies of this complex issue. What I said before was wrong, and I've corrected it now, and thanks go to all who cared enough to keep thinking, keep talking, and keep working on the issue." Dr. Geisler knows firsthand the value of cooperative apologetics.

Lack of Church Understanding

Most of us believe that our own church or denomination most closely mirrors biblical Christianity—after all, if we thought some other church was closer to the truth, we would probably join it! However, sometimes Christians confuse their own perspective with the mistaken idea that any belief or expression of Christianity with which they are unfamiliar is automatically heretical.

One Christian declared that he never pictures Christ when he prays and does not have pictures of Christ in his home. He explained that since we do not know what Jesus looked like, any picture is going to be inaccurate. If we look to any inaccurate picture when we think of or pray to Jesus, he reasoned, then we are not looking at the real Jesus but are actually worshiping a false Jesus! He warned strongly against such a practice that could tempt the believer to idolatry.

Evidently he did not realize that for much of church history the majority of believers were illiterate, and pictures were used to communicate or illustrate doctrinal truth, *not* to convey an accurate physical representation of Jesus. These "teaching pictures" (icons) communicated important doctrines to Christians who were not otherwise able to read the Scriptures. Because he failed to understand or appreciate other expressions of faith, he effectively cut off the majority of Christian believers of the past and present from valid faith and practice.

Obsession with Prophecy

Perhaps because of the strong biblical emphasis on the presence of false doctrine during the "end times," some Christians inadvertently promote their own personal views on the end times (eschatology) to the exclusion of any other Christian beliefs on the subject. All Christians throughout the centuries and throughout the world have believed the cardinal doctrine about Jesus' second coming. But the Church has never considered only one interpretation of the events surrounding the Second Coming as a determiner of orthodoxy and heresy. One caller to our radio show informed us that he knew the Lutheran church was a cult because he had attended a Lutheran Bible study and the teacher had said he did not think the idea of the pretribulational rapture was based on a good interpretation of Scripture! Regardless of one's eschatology, responsible Christians and churches have never made more than the simple fact of the Second Coming a test for orthodoxy.

Harold O. J. Brown, in his book *Heresies,* noted,

> The doctrine of the return of Christ . . . is one on which Christians have never come to substantial agreement. Orthodox believers all recognize that the Scripture teaches and the creeds affirm that Christ shall "come again to judge the living and the dead." But the time of his coming, and the signs that are to precede it, have been interpreted in several different ways.[2]

Lack of Comprehensive Research

Often students, in an effort to impress their professors, bury the text of their papers in a stockpile of footnotes and documentation and yet do not really know how to research and analyze their topics properly.

Sometimes researchers miss an important aspect of their topics and rely too much on just one kind of source or fail to dig below surface reports. A Christian researcher we know researched UFOs, but skipped some very important investigative and analysis procedures. He concluded from his studies of reported UFO sightings and contacts that almost all of them were demonic manifestations. But he had failed to investigate the background of most of the sensationalistic claims. Had he done so, as others have, he would have discovered that, though demonic activity may be able to manifest itself in that way, the majority of these sightings are clearly not demonic at all.[3]

Lack of Critical Thinking

Critical thinking is the ability to look at a situation or problem, understand its logical implications, and relate it to other situations or problems. Critical thinking is the ability to analyze an idea and compare it to known standards.

Because critical thinking is involved in almost all examination and analysis, mistakes in this area compose the majority of witch hunting techniques. One Christian writer counted the number of times a suspected author used terms assumed to be New Age and concluded that his overuse of the terminology was one of the proofs of his secret involvement in the New Age Movement. The argument was left to stand without any corroboration from looking at the context in which the writer used those terms. In fact, this Christian writer used more New Age terms in the critique than the original suspected author did!

Results of Witch Hunting

Inconsistent name calling and untestable accusations of heresy promote isolationism and pessimism in the Church. If we cannot have a clear standard for determining orthodoxy and heresy, then we are likely to be afraid of any contact with others for fear that we might unwittingly connect with a heretic. Christians become fearful that anything they think or do may be New Age or some other heresy in disguise. Christians who buy blanket condemnations cut themselves off from the rich variety of fellowship, practice, and belief that should be appreciated within the Body of Christ. And such Christians tend to retreat from relationships with other Christians and other churches for fear that they will be contaminated with heresy.

The Bible commands us to test all things, to hold fast to what is good, and to abhor what is evil (1 Thess. 5:21–22). True biblical discernment is an absolute necessity.

However, inadequate discernment is ineffective in championing truth and exposing error and runs the real risk of mislabeling truth as error and error as truth. In these days of deception, we cannot afford to have the wrong weapons (Eph. 6:10–17).

DEFICIENCIES OF WITCH HUNTING

In the following pages we will use Scripture to point out the deficiencies of witch hunting and provide the standards of biblical discernment. We will survey today's witch hunting trends and note their flaws, look at how some individuals and ministries have been hurt by witch hunting, and provide solid biblical principles for accurately upholding truth and exposing evil. By equipping ourselves with accurate biblical weapons, we can become active evangelists in the world, bringing the clear word of the gospel to a world in dying need of it.

The first step to our being able to appraise witch hunting accurately is to know the key doctrines of Christian orthodoxy. Without knowing what is orthodox, we cannot know the difference between what is genuinely heretical and what has been labeled falsely as heresy.

CHAPTER 2

Who Is Really Christian?

*O*ur friend sat across the kitchen table from us, slowly stirring his cup of coffee for the tenth time. He finally looked across at us, took a deep breath, and quietly declared, "I'm fed up with Christians. I've tried to become a part of three different churches over the last three years and for some reason I always picked the ones that were in the midst of splitting up over some stupid fight. It's just not worth it anymore. Maybe I won't go to church at all."

Keith expressed what a lot of us go through after the first bloom of our conversion to Christ has worn off and we begin to find out that Christians can argue and bicker just as skillfully as non-Christians about disagreements just as inane. His first church lost half its members when the pastor and most of the elders got "spirit-filled" and joined the charismatic movement. The second church did not really split, but Keith liked to refer to it as the "tithe reminder" church—not that the church emphasized offerings, but that 10 percent of the congregation did 90 percent of the work and activities. The 90 percenters, as Keith called them, complained that the 10 percenters were on a "works righteousness" trip and denied their salvation by their actions, if not their words. Of course, the 10 percenters were convinced that the 90 percenters were "shade-tree Christians." They liked to come in out of the sun, but they were not willing to commit themselves. Keith's third church had seemed better at first. No bickering, no cliques; everything appeared great. Then Keith began talking with some of the members. One elder was an alcoholic, but the church was considerate and compassionate and did not say anything to him because they did not want to hurt his feelings. They just kind of worked around him and did not schedule him for any elder duties before noon or after five. Another congregational leader declined to teach an adult Bible class because of his busy schedule, but he confided to Keith that he would have enjoyed helping a class learn to appreciate the "spiritual value" of the Bible in spite of its historical and scientific inaccuracies. Keith tried to stick it out—after all, the pastor loved God, upheld God's Word, and preached solid sermons. But he left when the congregation voted to close their soup kitchen serving the poor rather than come up with the extra money needed to pay the insurance increase. They could have paid the higher premium if they had canceled their thirtieth anniversary celebration at the country club, but everybody was looking forward to it.

"I don't doubt God," Keith assured us, "but who really is Christian? It doesn't make sense."

To answer Keith, we have to get behind appearances and fallible people. We have to look at the roots of Christian faith and practice.

A BIBLICAL FAITH

Christianity is distinct from world religions, cults, and other systems of belief. In Christianity both faith and fact are united. In Christianity we have the infinite invading the finite—God becoming man. Christianity does not call us to faith in spite of reason, but to reasonable faith. Christianity does not call us to faith instead of history, but to a historical faith. When the apostle Paul was brought to trial for preaching Jesus and his resurrection, he affirmed the historicity of the resurrection, challenging his captors to accept what they knew to be the truth:

> I am not mad, most noble Festus, but speak the words of truth and reason. For the king, before whom I also speak freely, knows these things; for I am convinced that none of these things escapes his attention, since this thing was not done in a corner (Acts 26:25–26).

Throughout the centuries, the Christian Church has preserved orthodoxy by never compromising the truth of the Scriptures, God's inerrant Word. When heresies and sects arose in the early Church, the leaders challenged them with Scripture. When false believers were cut off from the faith, it was on the authority of Scripture. When new believers were welcomed to Christ's Church, it was because they confessed scriptural faith and pledged their lives to its truth. Jesus petitioned the Father to "Sanctify them by Your truth. Your word is truth" (John 17:17).

TOLERANCE OR REBUKE?

There will always be differences of opinion within the Body of Christ (see Rom. 14, for example), but those differences of opinion can be tolerated only on peripheral issues, not on the core of the gospel. When Keith's third church, for example, condoned alcoholism, a lack of confidence in the Bible, and forsaking the poor, it was not tolerant, it was sinful. Scripture clearly commands the Church to rebuke heresy and immorality, not tolerate it.

First Thessalonians 5:21–22 commands us to test everything, clinging to what is good and true, rejecting absolutely what is evil. The Bereans in Acts 17:11 gave us the pattern for biblical discernment, testing everything by the Scriptures. Biblical discernment is not an option for Christians—it is a necessity.

On the other hand, false accusations, artificial standards, slander, and separation from true believers based on minor differences are all actions contrary to the Scriptures. *Witch hunting is using logic, Scripture, and/or evidence in the wrong ways in a futile effort to identify heresy and protect oneself or others from false belief.* Witch hunting is a dangerous practice. How many of these techniques does one have to practice before he imitates the pattern of Satan, who is called "the accuser of our brethren" (Rev. 12:10)? When does witch hunting degenerate into hating fellow believers?

> But know this, that in the last days perilous times will come: For men will be lovers of themselves, lovers of money, boasters, proud, blasphemers, disobedient to parents, unthankful, unholy, *unloving, unforgiving, slanderers,* without self-control, brutal, despisers of good, traitors, headstrong, haughty, lovers of pleasure rather than lovers of God, having a form of godliness but denying its power. And from such people turn away (2 Tim. 3:1–5, italics added for emphasis)!

Nobody wants to be a witch hunter, and armed with a good understanding of essential biblical doctrine, critical thinking ability, and a heart for biblical understanding, we can safely recognize the differences between error and truth without witch hunting. Not only will we be able to preserve ourselves from heresy and grow in biblical maturity, we will also be equipped "in humility correcting those who are in opposition, if God perhaps will grant them repentance, so that they may know the truth" (2 Tim. 2:25).

A GOOD UNDERSTANDING OF ESSENTIAL BIBLICAL DOCTRINE

The Bible sets out the standard for belief in five main doctrinal areas (1) God; (2) Jesus Christ; (3) man; (4) sin and salvation; and (5) Scripture. If anyone denies foundational and essential scriptural teachings in any of these five areas, he has placed himself outside of biblical faith.

By denial we mean that one is familiar with and understands the essentials of biblical faith but actively denies them. As the classical Princeton champion of orthodoxy J. Gresham Machen said, for example, concerning the virgin birth of Christ, "Never to have heard of the virgin birth is an entirely different thing from rejecting it after one has heard it attested by the New Testament books."[1] Another example comes from our own ministry. Once after a lecture Bob gave, a young woman asked him whether or not evolution was true. Bob spent almost half an hour explaining the scientific and philosophical shortcomings of the evolutionary theory. He packed an enormous amount of information into that thirty minutes and thoroughly trounced evolution.

He finished his answer, saying, "Not only does evolution fail the test of science and philosophy, most importantly, the Bible declares that God created everything and that Adam was his special creation, after his image. You can't believe the Bible is God's Word and still believe in evolution."

"*That's* exactly what I wanted to know," the young woman exclaimed. "I just became a Christian two days ago and I haven't had time yet to read the part of the Bible about creation. I didn't understand a word you said about all that science and philosophy stuff, but I won't believe in evolution anymore since the Bible is against it."

One places himself outside biblical faith when he *knows about* but *rejects* the clear teaching of Scripture in the five areas of belief listed above. But corollary to embracing or rejecting these central, essential biblical truths is the latitude allowed to imperfect, immature, still struggling Christians, as we all are to some extent.

Paul rebuked Peter for his hypocrisy in Galatians 2:11–21, but he did not call him a heretic. He rebuked the Galatians who were falling into legalism, but he did not tell them they were serving the antichrist. Paul rebuked the Corinthians for several sins, including toleration of immorality in their midst (1 Cor. 5:1–8) and failing to provide for the support of the Jerusalem saints (2 Cor. 9:1–15); but he did not accuse them of denying the faith. He warned Philemon to be kind to his wayward slave, but he did not threaten Philemon.

According to Scripture, we are to discern heresy accurately while at the same time maintaining a unity of faith based on patient brotherly love and true integrity (Rom. 14:12–20).

WHAT CHRISTIANS BELIEVE ABOUT GOD

The Bible summarizes the minimum necessary for belief in the true God of Scripture. We believe in only one God (Isa. 43:10; 1 Tim. 2:5); in the doctrine of the Trinity, that is, that within the nature of the one true God there are three eternal, distinct persons, the Father, the Son, and the Holy Spirit (Matt. 28:19); in God's sole ability to create from nothing (John 1:3; Rom. 4:17; Heb. 11:3); in his ongoing care and preservation of creation (Acts 17:25,28); and in his divine attributes, including his unique characteristics and his moral qualities.

The Bible describes God as triune (Luke 3:22); eternal, meaning without beginning or ending, uncreated (Isa. 40:28; Ex. 3:14); omnipotent, meaning that he has all power within his nature (Job 42:2); omniscient, meaning that he knows all things (Ps. 147:5); omnipresent, meaning that everything is immediately in his presence—it is impossible to escape his presence (Jer. 23:23–24); spirit, without a material body or form (John 4:24); and personal, with will, intellect, and decision-making ability (Ps. 94:9–10).

God's moral qualities are part of who he is, they are not independent standards to which he has decided to conform his actions. God is holy, set apart from his creation not only in the sense that he is uncreated, but also in a moral sense, without sin (Ps. 99:5,9); love (1 John 4:8,16); righteous and just, involving the purity of his nature, the entire freedom from his person of anything that is evil or tainted (Ps. 145:17; Zeph. 3:5); merciful, the union of his grace and justice through his lovingkindness (Ps. 86:15); and faithful, his promises always come true, he has absolute integrity (1 Cor. 1:9; 10:13; 1 John 1:9).

WHAT CHRISTIANS BELIEVE ABOUT JESUS CHRIST

We believe that Jesus Christ is truly God (John 1:1; Titus 2:13); truly man (Phil. 2:5–11); the second person of the Trinity (Matt. 28:19); personally distinct from both the Father (John 14:28) and the Holy Spirit (John 14:16); born of the Virgin Mary (Matt. 1:18; Luke 1:35); was born with a human nature, came in the flesh (John 1:14; 1 John 4:2–3); died for our sins (Acts 2:23); was resurrected from the dead on the third day (Acts 2:24) in his crucified, transformed body (Luke 24:39; John 20:27–28). After forty days of miraculous proofs of his bodily resurrection, he ascended into heaven (Acts 1:9–11); and will return to earth bodily (Acts 1:11; Titus 2:13; Rev. 1:7) to judge those living and those dead (Matt. 25:31–46). We believe that Jesus Christ is holy (Mark 1:24; Acts 3:14); loving—both to the Father and Spirit, and to us (John 14:21); compassionate (Mark 6:34; John 6:37); and humble (Phil. 2:1–11).

WHAT CHRISTIANS BELIEVE ABOUT MAN

Man was created by God and is uniquely in God's image (Gen. 1:26). To be made in God's image includes being personal, having will, intellect, and decision-making ability, and the capacity for love—covenantal commitment. Man was perfect when he was created by God, and he enjoyed fellowship with God (Rom. 5:12,14). Man fell into sin by his own choice (Gen. 3), and individually and corporately is unable in himself to restore his relationship with

God (Rom. 3:23; 5:14). Man is not divine (Isa. 31:3; 47:8–11). Man's destiny without the intervention of Christ's death on the cross is eternal separation from the loving presence of God (Matt. 25:46). Believers, who have been redeemed from sin by the power of the Holy Spirit—justification (Romans 3:23–24), are assured of God's continual sustaining, enabling, and loving presence in their earthly lives—sanctification (John 10:25–30; Phil. 1:6; Heb. 10:38–39); and God's eternal, loving communion in their lives after death—glorification (Rom. 8:11,21,30).

WHAT CHRISTIANS BELIEVE ABOUT SIN AND SALVATION

As we already stated, man apart from Christ is hopelessly mired in sin (Rom. 3:10–18). Man cannot reach out to God on his own initiative (2 Tim. 1:9). Since it is our sin which separates us from God, it is God who must reach out to us in reconciliation. He has done this—called the atonement (Heb. 9:22) through the death of his Son (Rom. 5:8) on the cross (Heb. 9:14). This reconciles us to God—justification (Rom. 3:24–25), without any attempt on our part to earn it (Rom. 3:26–30; Eph. 2:8–10), responding freely by his grace and calling (John 1:12).

WHAT CHRISTIANS BELIEVE ABOUT SCRIPTURE

When Christians use the word *Scripture,* we mean the Old and New Testaments as the divinely authoritative, inerrant Word of God (2 Tim. 3:16). Jesus Christ validated the Old Testament (Luke 24:27–47) and assured us of the trustworthiness of the New Testament (John 14:26). Man cannot add to the Bible without being revealed a liar (Prov.

30:5–6). Anything which claims to be the gospel, but which denies the biblical gospel is cursed (Gal. 1:6–8). The Bible is God's Word (Heb. 4:12), the Word of truth (James 1:18), and the sword of the Spirit (Eph. 6:17). We can depend on the Bible (1 Peter 4:11) without reservation in all matters on which it touches.[2]

THE UNITY OF FAITH

What does all this dry theology have to do with contemporary Christian faith? A Christian friend of ours was in Beijing, China during the student demonstrations and massacre in the late spring of 1989. Our family prayed for him as each day our television news showed the demonstrations escalating and the government moving closer to violence. We knew Kevin was in special danger as an American, a Christian, a student, and the fiancé of a Chinese Christian. Finally we received an airmail letter from him. He and his fiancée were safe! He shared in his letter how that time of unrest and uncertainty was an opportunity for evangelism. "My [fiancée's Chinese cousin] said recently that she now believes in Jesus. . . . She is quite moved by the loving support Christians have given the students. . . . Christians have given food and donated money to help them. She is impressed by an ethic based on love and unselfishness." Kevin went on to write that another family member had scoffed, declaring that "the people (masses) are God. . . . Science is the instrument of salvation." Kevin's response was that no matter how hard someone worked and no matter how many people worked together, no one could make a lie turn into truth. Christians are not just nice people—they are people who are nice *because they have the truth.*

No matter what an alternative belief system (cultic, occultic, or even atheistic) offers to a potential convert, if it is good, Christianity offers it too—plus what the others can *never* deliver, the truth of God incarnate. These doctrines just described are not just a bunch of boring words, they are life-giving truths!

Because of this unity of faith, Christians all over the world can meet in unity and peace, together showing the world, even the godless world of Communism, the love which comes from Christ, who is himself truth (John 14:6).

Kevin knows firsthand the value of a unified faith that could bring him into fellowship with a young woman around the world and from another culture and language. He knows firsthand the value of Christians so committed to truth that they are willing to risk their lives to help students struggling for freedom under a totalitarian government. And Kevin also knows firsthand the value of truth, what corresponds to reality rather than what sounds like a good story. You see, before Kevin became a Christian, he was in a cult. As a young Jehovah's Witness he used to call us from New York every Tuesday evening to argue about doctrine. He now knows the truth of God's Word, and God has used him to spread the good news of the gospel to the far reaches of China.

This is not the forum for a lengthy theology lesson. What we have provided is an outline of scriptural teaching on the essentials.[3] But you can see from Kevin's story that a firm foundation gives a Christian the strength and power to share the gospel with assurance, to really make a difference in one's own world for Jesus Christ.

The Bible is God's perfect revelation to mankind, containing all anyone needs for salvation and sanctification (2 Pet. 1:3–4; 2 Tim. 2:15). From the Scriptures Christians have always derived the essentials of orthodox faith. Anyone who denies any of these doctrines denies the teachings of Christ.

On the other hand, diversity of opinion on nonessential issues is permissible and should not divide believers (Ps. 133:1–3). Nonessential doctrines concern specifics about the order of worship in the church; the mode of water baptism; the frequency of offering communion; the extent to which Christians should be involved in social activism; whether or not alcoholic beverages can be used judiciously. Thinking, studying, and talking about the nonessentials from a biblical basis can help us grow in Christian maturity. But using unity on nonessentials as a test for orthodoxy is not a good idea (Rom. 14).

A biblical discerner distinguishes between heresy and ignorance, between apostasy and error. A biblical discerner never compromises on essential doctrine, but graciously loves and supports other Christians who differ on peripheral issues (Rom. 15:14; Gal. 6:1).

QUALIFICATIONS FOR BIBLICAL DISCERNMENT

When our staff intern, Joe, first started working with us, he wanted to be sure we understood that he was no theologian. "I don't know what epistemology is, I have never met an anarthrous predicate nominative, and I use my one-volume systematic theology as a doorstop. I can't do all that intellectual argumentation you guys do, but I want to help people know the real Jesus." Joe confused academic prowess and erudite vocabulary with mature biblical understanding. He was convinced he did not have the qualifications for being an apologist, but over the weeks we saw that he had the only qualifications necessary: he loved God, he knew what the Bible said, and he cared about truth. The night he prayed with a young Jehovah's Witness to receive Christ, he did not define epistemology, he did not talk about New Testament Greek, and he did not even use the word *theology*. But he carefully and compassionately shared the truth of God's Word in words the Jehovah's Witness could understand. Joe did not have a graduate degree and he was not ordained, but he had taken the time, effort, and self-discipline to learn how to think, understand God's Word, and tell the difference between truth and lies. He had proved he was a biblical discerner.

Have a Sound Theological Background

Even though Joe used his theology book as a door-stop, he had a sound theological background. He clearly learned the biblical teachings on all the major doctrines. He was familiar with what other apologists had to say on controversial subjects. He recognized that "in the multitude of counselors there is safety" (Prov. 11:14), and so he checked out his ideas with others who were committed to teaching biblical truth too. He did not reject their opinions without persuasive, reasonable, and scriptural reasons.

Be Familiar with Historical and Contemporary Varieties of Christianity

A good biblical discerner is also familiar with both historical and contemporary varieties of Christianity. He is able to distinguish doctrinally between varieties of Christianity and outright cults or sects. While he does not have to agree with every form of Christian expression, practice, or minor doctrinal difference, he respects what is within scriptural and historical orthodoxy. This is especially important in the area of eschatology (end times), which seems to engender more fighting and emotional accusations than other topics.

Good apologists recognize that peripheral doctrines should not be used as litmus tests of orthodoxy. These include (but are not limited to) forms of worship, prayer, church government, and the relationship between the Church and the world (as long as there is not compromise with the world on essential doctrines).

Able to Distinguish Between Different Religious Ideas That Sound Similar

Before you trust someone who claims to be able to divide the heretics from the orthodox, be sure he demonstrates a familiarity with the major world religions and their worldviews. He should be able to trace the source of faulty beliefs accurately if they derive from non-Christian religions. He should be able to distinguish between different religious ideas that sound similar. For example, both Mormonism and an aspect of Hindu thought teaches that man can become God. However, the Mormons do not get their teaching from the older Hindu teaching, which contradicts Mormon theology in that it is pantheistic—God is the impersonal all, rather than henotheistic—one personal god is worshiped among the many in existence. Just because both the Hindu and the Mormon say, "Man can become God," one cannot necessarily conclude that both teachings are the same, come from a common source, or one comes from the other.

Able to Compare and Contrast Conflicting Sources and Opinions

Many people who set themselves up as biblical discerners expect their readers or listeners to believe their conclusions despite the fact that they have not followed recognized standards of comprehensive, balanced research. This means comparing and contrasting conflicting sources and opinions. It also means understanding what various writers and speakers meant, not just what their words allow for or what they mean when used by somebody else. We read a book by an ex-cultist that detailed what life was like for someone in this cult. The ex-cultist was the daughter of the founder of the cult. The experiences, teachings, and worldview she related did not match what typical members of that cult had experienced. It was not that she was wrong about what had happened to her, it's that her experience was not typical. By presenting it as such, other members (and ex-members) are misled.

Here's another example. A researcher called us to test out his explanation of a particular occultic phenomenon with us. After he carefully explained how he reconciled this aberration with Scripture, we asked, "Have you checked the sources that originally reported the occultic activity?" He had not. And, unfortunately for him, his hours of theological and biblical research turned out to be useless for this event—his further research showed that the "occultic phenomenon" was actually a fraud perpetrated by a family who wanted to win a tabloid newspaper's contest for the best occultic manifestation-of-the-year award. Comprehensive research means building a solid, well-reasoned case from multiple sources before administering wholesale criticism.

Practice Effective Critical-Thinking Methods

The one you trust to tell you what is biblical and what is heretical should practice effective critical-thinking methods. He should not fall for simple logical fallacies like those discussed in this book—appealing to inappropriate authority, guilt by association, term switching, source fallacy.[4]

It is usually much easier to see these logical inconsistencies when the subject does not concern our vital life commitments. We merely chuckle, for example, when a television commercial confuses terms in a deliberate attempt to convince us its product is best: "Studies have shown that———aspirin was better at reducing postpartum pain than any other standard pain reliever. . . . So the next time you have a *headache,* take———aspirin!" But we seem reluctant to surrender some of our prized religious commitments, even when those commitments are based on a confusion of terms or other logical inconsistency.

We once talked with a young Christian named Mary who had what she believed was an unanswerable logical problem with the goodness of God. After we had given her three good, logical, biblical answers to the problem she responded, "You can't answer this! How can I continue to live by *faith* if everything is *reasonable?*" She had confused the meaning of the term *faith.* It does not mean to believe in spite of the evidence or in the face of logical contradiction, but it does mean confidence in the testimony of God and his Word. Mary's maturity in Christ and peace with God increased dramatically when she began practicing good biblical discernment.

If we commit ourselves to biblical discernment, we will safeguard the purity of our faith (Jude 3) while at the same time ensure the unity of Christ in love (1 Cor. 12:25–26). The essential doctrines upon which we base our judgment of orthodoxy and heresy also have been summarized by Christians throughout the centuries. These summaries, called creeds, provided them and still provide us with accurate measuring rods for biblical accuracy.

CONFESSIONS

Credo is the Latin term for "I believe." Everyone believes something; everyone has a creed. The question facing us today is, Which "creed" truly represents biblical faith? Throughout Church history, Christians have faced questions concerning orthodoxy and heresy and they developed creeds as formal expressions of their answers. These creeds, based on Scripture and grown out of controversy, have stood as bulwarks against heresy.

We became Christians during the Jesus Movement of the late 1960s and early 1970s, and like many "Jesus People," we had little familiarity with Church history or organized Christianity. Gretchen grew up in a liberal Methodist church. When she became a Christian and gave an emotional testimony at a youth group meeting, the youth pastor patted her on the shoulder and said, "That's okay. You'll feel better in a few days." Bob grew up as a nominal Catholic. His Italian family figured Catholicism was like spaghetti—all Italians had it. Both of us were *proud* that we had "found Jesus" outside of "dead and dull church-ianity." With the unique naiveté of baby-boomer young adulthood, we and thousands of our brothers and sisters in Christ were convinced that we were the epitome of all true born-again Christians. After all, our births had proved there was life after World War II. Our protests had stopped the Vietnam War. (Remember the lyric, "War. What is it good for? Absolutely nothing."?) Our conversions had initiated the outpouring of the Holy Spirit "in those last days" (a dubious fulfillment of Joel 2:28–32). And *our* generation would not "pass away" before the great Rapture, the Tribulation, and the Battle of Armageddon. Being a Christian couldn't get any better!

Well, twenty years and a lot of Bible study has tempered our self-absorption. We may be the baby-boomers, but our generation is busy right now killing fully one-third of our own babies through abortion each year. And none of "our boys" are dying in Vietnam, but thousands, perhaps millions, of Vietnamese have died experiencing the "liberation" of the Communist victors. The great movement named after the Holy Spirit produced more than just spirituality. It produced Jim and Tammy Bakker and Jimmy Swaggart. And the Rapture? We have a friend who just turned forty, has never held a full-time job, never married, and is homeless because he does not have time for a normal life. After all, Jesus is coming soon!

Has God failed? No. But our meager understanding of his plans and our inconsistent commitments have failed. We were so busy being the world's best Christians that we tended not to notice that "we are surrounded by so great a cloud of witnesses" (Heb. 12:1), Christians and believers from both biblical times and church history who have already fought "the good fight of faith" and have already laid "hold on eternal life" (1 Tim. 6:12). Throughout history God has had faithful servants who have been intimately acquainted with his Word and his Spirit, and Christians today cannot afford to ignore the tremendous contributions they made to the integrity of our faith. The creeds summarize the historic answer of the Church to heresy through the life-giving words of Scripture. After we had spent hundreds of hours studying God's Word to understand basic Christian doctrine, we discovered that our ancestors in the faith had already provided us with cogent and concise explanations of scriptural truth.

PRESERVING THE FAITH

The creeds are not substitutes for Scripture, but they summarize Scripture and set scriptural truth in contrast to heresy. The Apostles' Creed is one of our earliest statements of Christian faith outside the New Testament.

Some historians make a good case that Philippians 2:5–11 is Paul's inspired recitation of an early creed, predating A.D. 61. Matthew 16:16 and 28:19 are also creedal in nature. And Romans 10:9–10 reminds us, "If you confess with your mouth the Lord Jesus and believe in your heart that God has raised Him from the dead, you will be saved. For with the heart one believes to righteousness, and with the mouth confession is made to salvation."

The Apostles' Creed was used in the very early Church to test the orthodoxy of one's faith and, in question (catechal) form, to approve those who wished to join the body of faith.

The Apostles' Creed[5]

I believe in God the Father Almighty
Maker of heaven and earth.
I believe in Jesus Christ His Only Son, our Lord
Who was conceived by the Holy Ghost,
Born of the Virgin Mary,
Suffered under Pontius Pilate,
Was crucified, dead, and buried;

He descended into hell;
The third day He rose again from the dead;
He ascended into heaven,
And sitteth on the right hand
Of God the Father Almighty;
From thence He shall come
To judge the quick and the dead.

I believe in the Holy Ghost;
The holy Christian [catholic] Church,
The communion of saints;
The forgiveness of sins;
The resurrection of the body;
And the life everlasting.
Amen.

The Nicene Creed, developed from the Council of Nicea around A.D. 325, expanded on the Apostles' Creed, carefully distinguishing biblical Christian doctrine from the heresies of those who denied the deity of Christ and the Holy Spirit. It was formulated in response to the challenge of heresy. The precise but complicated statements concerning the person and work of Christ responded to the controversy raging at the time over whether or not Christ was created. Since it is the Holy Spirit's ministry to testify of Christ (John 16:14), the earliest Christians did not formulate an extensive theology concerning him. But by the time of the Nicene Creed, his personhood and deity had both been challenged by heretics, and this creed responded clearly and authoritatively.

The Nicene Creed[6]

I believe in one God the Father Almighty,
Maker of heaven and earth,
And of all things visible and invisible:

And in one Lord Jesus Christ, the only-
    begotten Son of God;
Begotten of His Father before all worlds,
God of God, Light of Light, Very God of Very
    God;
Begotten, not made;
Being of one substance with the Father;
By whom all things were made:
Who for us men and for our salvation came
    down from heaven,
And was incarnate by the Holy Ghost of the
    Virgin Mary,
And was made man:
And was crucified also for us under Pontius
    Pilate;
He suffered and was buried:
And the third day he rose again according to
    the Scriptures:
And ascended into heaven,
And sitteth on the right hand of the Father:
And he shall come again, with glory, to judge
    both the quick and the dead;
Whose kingdom shall have no end.

And I believe in the Holy Ghost, the Lord and
    Giver of Life,
Who proceedeth from the Father and the Son;
Who with the Father and Son together is
    worshipped and glorified;
Who spake by the Prophets:

> And I believe in the one catholic and Apostolic
>   Church:
> I acknowledge one Baptism for the remission
>   of sins:
> And I look for the Resurrection of the dead:
> And the life of the world to come.
> Amen.

These two creeds and those that developed later concentrated on the same central truths, amplified and clarified in opposition to particular contemporary heresies. For example, all affirmed the second coming of Christ, but none dictated when and how that coming would occur.[7]

When one's faith is divorced from a reasonable understanding of biblical doctrine, he has no objective measuring rod for testing his own faith or the faith of others. How can he tell what is biblical? How can he tell what is heretical? It's fine to say, "just trust the Bible," but as soon as you read, understand, and summarize (even for yourself) the essential teachings of the Bible, you have formed a creed. Sadly, contemporary Christians too often abandon serious study of God's Word to concentrate on titillating spiritual cliches.

> Conservative Christians cannot escape from the charge that they have replaced instruction in the things of God with religious entertainment, and that the doctrinal backbone to their preaching is decidedly weak. Many have no idea that creeds and confessions are an essential aid to Christian growth, and that the quality of our spiritual life is directly dependent on our understanding of spiritual truth. They do not know that the great centuries of the Church have been marked not by an aversion to doctrine and theological controversy, but by a passion for these things.

Of course controversy can be unpleasant and divisive, but the New Testament is full of it, and the great arguments of the past have seldom diminished our respect for the truths for which men fought and died. Conservative Christians need to recover a sense of their heritage, both in order to be able to defend it more intelligently and in order to be able to enjoy it as a living reality in their spiritual experience today.[8]

Creedal faith is *living* faith—faith that is nourished by God's Word and which produces the fruit of a life consecrated to biblical truth.

This is the origin of Christian symbols or creeds. They never precede faith, but presuppose it. They emanate from the inner life of the Church, independently of external occasion. There would have been creeds even if there had been no doctrinal controversies. In a certain sense it may be said that the Christian Church has never been without a creed. . . . The baptismal formula and the words of institution of the Lord's Supper are creeds. . . . The Church is, indeed, not founded on symbols, but on Christ; not on any words of man, but on the word of God; yet it is founded on Christ as confessed by men, and a creed is man's answer to Christ's question, man's acceptance and interpretation of God's word. . . . Where there is faith, there is also profession of faith. As "faith without works is dead," so it may be said also that faith without confession is dead.[9]

Remember the popularized version of the challenge to good works, "If you were brought to trial for being a Christian, would there be enough evidence to convict you?" We could add to that, "If you were put on the stand to testify, would you know what to say?"

CHAPTER 3

Errors That Create Witch Hunters

*T*he epistle of James contains advice as important today as it was nearly two thousand years ago: "My brethren, let not many of you become teachers, knowing that we shall receive a stricter judgment. For we all stumble in many things. If anyone does not stumble in word, he is a perfect man, able also to bridle the whole body" (James 3:1–2).

It is hard to be a teacher or leader in the Church. None of us are perfect; as teachers and leaders we are imperfect people dealing with other imperfect people in imperfect churches in an imperfect world. The wonder is not that we have so many differences; but that, by the power of the Holy Spirit, we have such unity as Christians. None of us are exempt from criticism. We have made mistakes and will continue to make mistakes throughout our lifetimes. But even though we cannot be perfect in this life, the Scriptures command us to continue maturing *toward* that perfection which will only be ours at the last day (Matt. 5:48). Christians can be confident that "He who has begun a good work in you will complete it until the day of Jesus Christ" (Phil. 1:6).

Part of that maturing process is learning to tell the difference between right and wrong, truth and error, orthodoxy and heresy, good and evil. Biblical discernment is every believer's responsibility to God (Phil. 1:9–11), to other Christians (Acts 17:11), and to the world (1 Pet. 3:15–16).

One young intern, Roger, began working with us several years ago. He had memorized most of Walter Martin's taped messages, he was in Bible college, and he was sure he was God's gift to apologetics. He worked with us for several months, listening as we answered people's questions on the phone, going with us to witness to cultists, and participating in our everyday ministering to others. Then we asked him to answer a letter from a mother whose adult daughter was in a cult. The mother herself was mixed up not only about the teaching of this cult, but also about her own Christian faith. She desperately needed help. Roger came back frustrated the next day, letter in hand. He had a hard time getting started, but finally, sheepishly, he muttered, "I don't think I can answer this letter. I've got all the facts and information, but she needs more than that. She needs to learn how to think straight. She needs to know somebody who cares about her and will encourage her to do what's right. I don't know how to do that!" Roger was beginning to learn the difference between knowledge and wisdom. He was also learning the responsibility of one Christian to another and to nonbelievers. Along the way, he also learned the most common mistakes Christians make in understanding both how to defend the faith and how to express that faith persuasively to others (apologetics). Below are the four most common problems of witch hunting, problems Roger learned to avoid as he matured. While these are four common problems of witch hunting, it would be a mistake to apply this profile wholly to any particular individual. Remember, anyone who seeks to discern truth from error is vulnerable to using witch hunting techniques. Only as we draw close to the Lord; prepare ourselves more and more with reasonable, scripturally sound principles; and think carefully and cautiously, will we gain a measure of protection against using witch hunting tactics.

WITCH HUNTING DISCREDITS MANY EXPRESSIONS OF CHRISTIANITY

One prevalent witch hunting problem is a lack of understanding or appreciation of church history or of expressions of Christianity outside our own denominational niches. It is true that all orthodox Christians throughout history and in all the denominations agree on the essentials of biblical doctrine. But even in New Testament times Christians had varieties of expression for their faith, different kinds of church structure, and different understandings concerning peripheral areas of belief and practice.

The apostles Peter and James concentrated on evangelizing the Jews. The apostle Paul and his co-workers Barnabas and Timothy took the gospel to the Gentiles. Jewish Christians had a great concern for ritual, and Gentile Christians often lacked sensitivity to those concerns (Acts 15). Many New Testament Christians held varying speculative views about end-time prophecies since the apostles were often given cryptic answers by Jesus to their questions about when and how he would return. Some early Christians shared their possessions and assets (Acts 4:32–35).

Over the centuries the Church diversified as different cultures were evangelized around the world. As a result, various traditions and forms of church government gained precedence in different areas. It is true that sometimes pagan practices or beliefs that are truly *incompatible* with the Bible crept into local churches; there were heresies, there were excesses, there were mistakes. But, by and large, the premedieval Church maintained the essentials of biblical doctrine and its internal distinctives developed within respect for orthodoxy.

For example, teaching pictures (icons) proliferated in the Church, not as excuses for idol worship, but as vehicles for teaching doctrine to illiterate congregations. In the Western Church three-dimensional icons were used as well as two-dimensional ones, while the Eastern Church always emphasized pictures and eventually banned any iconic use of statues. Of course, there were the spiritually blind who worshiped icons, but that was not the purpose of icons in the Church. Eastern Orthodox authority Anthony M. Coniaris notes, "The purpose of icons is three-fold: (1) to create reverence in worship; (2) to instruct those who are unable to read; (3) to serve as a . . . link between the worshipper and God."[1]

In A.D. 1054 the Western and Eastern churches broke fellowship and communion and became the Roman Catholic and Eastern Orthodox churches. Today's Eastern Orthodox churches maintain the same forms of worship, ecclesiastical (church) structure and rules, and doctrinal stance as did their forebears more than one thousand years ago. This reflects their own view of orthodoxy and their commitment to one way of preserving it.

The Roman Catholic Church, partly because of its commitment to the apostolic authority of the ongoing Church, allowed significant deviation within its structure. This gave rise to the brilliant philosophical theologies of Thomas Aquinas and other prominent Catholic theologians. But it also permitted unorthodox and abusive practices and beliefs in the medieval Church. (Martin Luther, for example, was spurred to protest the problems within the Roman Church partly because of the unbiblical selling of indulgences as a way of enriching the Vatican coffers.) Some of those practices and beliefs are still evident in parts of the Roman Catholic Church today. (The Santeria cult, for example, tries to combine the Roman veneration of the saints with African animistic polytheism.)

The Reformation constituted the first major break of fellowship and authority in the Western Church. With no single authority structure or leadership, the Reformation fostered even more diversity in the Body of Christ. The Lutheran tradition emphasized certain interpretations concerning the atonement, the sacraments, and church government. Other Reformers followed in the tradition of John Calvin, whose distinctive interpretations of the atonement are today refined and referred to as Calvinism. The Arminian tradition embraced anabaptist groups which emphasized, among other things, the general withdrawal of the Church from the affairs of this world. In England the Anglican church arose as a protest to the sovereignty of the Roman pope, but differed little in structure or practice from Roman Catholicism.

The church in America expanded on the diversity begun in the Reformation. The colonies contained settlements of Roman Catholics, Puritans, Anglicans, Calvinists, Arminians, Inner Light groups (Friends, etc.), and Baptists.

Today American Christianity is as diverse as the American population. Anybody can start a new church, and there are literally hundreds of denominations nationwide. There are even groups of churches with common roots, beliefs, and practices that function together but refuse to call themselves denominations out of a dislike for the negative connotations they perceive with the word.

There are only two main ingredients that provide unity in the midst of this great Christian diversity: (1) fidelity to essential biblical doctrine and (2) a common commitment to Jesus Christ in individual salvation experience. We have spoken and worshiped in churches across America. We have praised God with Vietnamese Christians even though we could only communicate through translators. We spoke at an Armenian Christian church where we did not understand the words to the songs but felt at home with our common faith. We talk with Baptists about being born again, Lutherans about being drawn by the Holy Spirit, and Reformed Christians about being predestined. Within American Christianity there is a richness of perspective and culture that enhances rather than detracts from serving the Lord.

This is just a thumbnail sketch of the growth in Christian diversity, but it serves to illustrate a point: When one begins to view his own expression of Christianity as the only valid one, he excludes thousands of churches and millions of believers both today and throughout the history of the Church.[2]

Witch hunting fails to consider the diversity within Christianity. By diversity we do not mean ecumenism, compromise, or carnality. We mean honest difference of opinion, belief, or practice in nonessential areas. These differences typically arise from different cultural backgrounds and in areas where the Scriptures are largely silent or ambiguous.

Texe Marrs's *Dark Secrets of the New Age* has one whole chapter devoted to "Apostasy: Takeover of the Christian Church" in which he catalogs a variety of examples of what he calls apostasy within the American Christian Church.[3] Here is the "proof" he provides of the *apostasy* of the Presbyterian Church (U.S.A.):

> The leadership of the Presbyterian Church (U.S.A.) repeatedly has branded the U.S. government as a warmonger. Its Advisory Council on Church and Society recently published a study which promotes pacifist resistance to the government and calls on its members to withdraw from military-related occupations and refuse to serve in military service. Opinion polls show that rank-and-file Presbyterians strongly disapprove of their Church's stance, but its activist hierarchy has seized control and continues its broadsides against America.[4]

Marrs is not just disagreeing with the Presbyterians, he is using this as proof of its *apostasy*. Marrs's own doctrinal biases are clear. We probably agree with Marrs that absolute pacifism is not biblical, and that church government should have at least some democratic elements. However, to *prove* Presbyterian apostasy by pointing to pacifism and the Presbyterian Church's leadership ignoring the views of its lay members is not fair. We would agree that some leaders within the Presbyterian Church (U.S.A.) are in apostasy for different reasons: It compromises essential biblical doctrines, in particular the inerrancy of God's Word, the absolute and unique deity of Christ, his bodily resurrection, salvation by grace alone, and the exclusivity of Christianity.[5]

Disagreement over nonessential doctrines does not properly or biblically distinguish between the orthodox and the apostate. Such intolerance not only condemns orthodox believers with differing viewpoints, but also condemns the apostate for the wrong reasons, leaving them opportunity to avoid valid charges of apostasy by debunking the false charges.

WITCH HUNTING IS OFTEN INTOLERANT OF ALTERNATE ESCHATOLOGIES

Eschatology, or the study of end times, is one of the largest areas of diversity in the Church today and is one of areas most vulnerable to witch hunting. The Church has always been united in belief in Christ's second coming. This event is related in all of the authoritative creeds of the Church and is clearly and unequivocally taught in the New Testament. However, the timing and manner of his return is not nearly so clear as some contemporary writers make it appear.

There are three major eschatological views prevalent in the Church today: (1) *amillennialism,* which teaches that the millennial reign of Christ is not literal and can be related to what takes place in the believer's heart beginning at conversion, Christ's physical return at the time of the judgment, resurrection, and reconciliation of all things; (2) *postmillennialism,* which teaches that the millennial reign of Christ will be through the Church as his representative on the earth, Christ's physical return at the end of the millennium; and (3) *premillennialism,* which teaches that Christ's second coming will occur before the earthly millennium and that during it Christ will rule visibly from Jerusalem. Within premillennialism there are three major positions concerning the seven-year "Great Tribulation": (1) *dispensational pretribulationism,* which teaches that the Church will be "raptured" out of the earth before the Great Tribulation starts; (2) *midtribulationism,* which teaches that the Church will be raptured during the Great Tribulation but just before the punishment of God afflicts the world; and (3) *posttribulationism* (usually referred to as *historic premillennialism*), which teaches that the Church will meet Christ at his second coming after the Great Tribulation, much as officials go out to meet a coming dignitary and escort him into their jurisdiction.

Each of these eschatological positions has able defenders within evangelical Christianity. Each attempts to make a cohesive picture of future events from prophecies and Scriptures in accord with God's demonstrated nature and actions toward man. Each attempts to uphold the integrity of God's Word and the revealed character of God.

But the differences among these views points out the lack of comprehensive biblical data on the subject. Approximately 27 percent (one-quarter) of the Bible's verses are prophetic.[6] But only eighty-eight of those verses, or less than 3 percent of the Bible, deal with end-time prophecies, those referring to a time after the New Testament times.[7] It should not be surprising to us, based on the scarcity of scriptural detail (and its symbolism), that there is disagreement within orthodoxy concerning eschatology.

However, witch hunting usually assumes and propagates *one* viewpoint as the only valid interpretation of prophecy. For example, Dave Hunt, in *Beyond Seduction,* disparages any eschatological interpretation other than his own.[8] He summarizes his view of the end as though it is the only view one could reasonably conclude from Scripture:

> How could the church be expected to establish the kingdom by taking over the world when even God cannot accomplish that without violating man's freedom of choice? During His thousand-year reign, Christ will visibly rule the world in perfect righteousness from Jerusalem and will impose peace upon all nations. Satan will be locked up, robbed of the power to tempt. . . . Yet at the end of the thousand years, when Satan is released, millions of those who have experienced . . . Christ's perfect reign all their lives will be deceived, just as Eve was. Converging from all over the world to war against Christ and the saints at Jerusalem, these rebels will finally have to be banished from God's presence forever (Revelation 20:7–10).[9]

By not even mentioning other valid interpretations (even within Hunt's dispensational camp) in his own recitation of the end-time scenario, he effectively dismisses them, rejecting them as viable alternate explanations. He shows no consideration for his readers who may not be aware that other options exist, and no consideration for Christians who believe those optional viewpoints. This is unfair. Millions of Christians through the centuries have held other views. Hunt may not agree with them, but they and Hunt's readers at least deserve his acknowledgment of their existence within orthodoxy.

WITCH HUNTING IGNORES OTHER LEADERS

Another unfortunate side effect of having to teach ourselves much of cult apologetics during the 1970s was that we were often isolated. Most Christians did not understand our commitment (they sometimes even termed it fanaticism), a commitment which seemed to be compelling us to engage in dialogue with every cultist and other nonbeliever we met. And since most of our favorite apologists wrote from fifty to nineteen hundred years ago, we met them only through their books. We really did not have much opportunity to grow from our contemporaries who were more seasoned in the Lord.

Some Christians unfortunately never learn to test themselves with other leaders in the faith. It is all too easy to separate oneself from other church leaders and organizations and from other biblical discernment ministries. This results in little or no interaction with established apologetic ministries.

There is nothing magic or perfect about established churches, leaders, or experts. Giving one a title, a Ph.D., or a clerical collar does not make him or her infallible. However, as we shall see, the Bible clearly teaches respect for elders, the importance of church counsel, and the wisdom of consulting one's peers. There are numerous admonishments concerning this in Scripture and multiple examples of both the blessings attendant upon those who follow this principle and the problems for those who ignore it.

Biblical Accountability

Moses argued for his people's freedom before the mighty pharaoh, led his people out of Egypt into Sinai, and represented God's will to them. But Moses realized he didn't know everything. He still had respect for others' maturity. He respected his father-in-law, Jethro, asking Jethro's permission to go back to Egypt to rescue his people (Ex. 4:18) and even taking Jethro's spiritual advice in the wilderness. Jethro served the true God (Ex. 18:11–12), and God used him to counsel Moses about how best to serve his people, who were exhausting Moses with their complaints and disputes.

> So Moses' father-in-law said to him, "The thing that you do is not good. Both you and these people who are with you will surely wear yourselves out. For this thing is too much for you; you are not able to perform it by yourself. Listen now to my voice; I will give you counsel, and God will be with you. . . .
> So Moses heeded the voice of his father-in-law and did all that he had said (Ex. 18:17–19,24).

The apostle Paul did not disdain other leaders either. He met the risen Lord on the road to Damascus in one of the most dramatic conversion stories in the New Testament. He was taught personally by the Lord in the desert for three years. His early ministry was characterized by strong teaching and successful evangelism. He knew that God had called him to be an apostle of equal status to Peter, James, and the others. And yet he still submitted his calling to those who were already acknowledged as the leaders in the Church:

> Then after fourteen years I went up again to Jerusalem with Barnabas, and also took Titus with me. And I went up by revelation, and communicated to them that gospel which I preach among the Gentiles, but privately to those who were of reputation, lest by any means I might run, or had run, in vain (Gal. 2:1–2).

Paul also sought the advice of the Jerusalem leaders concerning the Gentile believers' accommodations of Jewish believers' customs (Acts 15:2).

We are not advocating blind submission to church leaders or blind acceptance of the sometimes faulty teaching of other discernment leaders. Even Paul conditioned his statement that Christians should "be imitators of me" with *"just as I also imitate Christ"* (1 Cor. 11:1, italics added). We should not be isolated permanently from established, confirmed apologetics ministries. Rather, we should take their views and advice seriously, carefully considering them before we espouse opposing views.

Paul was advised by several churches (Acts 21:4, 10–14) not to go to Jerusalem because he would be imprisoned there. He listened to their advice respectfully, considered carefully his decision, and respected their role in leadership. He chose to go against their advice, but explained his reasoning and affirmed his common faith with them:

> And see, now I go bound in the spirit to Jerusalem, not knowing the things that will happen to me there, except that the Holy Spirit testifies in every city, saying that chains and tribulations await me. But none of these things move me; nor do I count my life dear to myself, so that I may finish my race with joy, and the ministry which I received from the Lord Jesus, to testify to the gospel of the grace of God (Acts 20:22–24).

First Peter 5:1–3 presents the balance between leadership authority and humility, contrasting willingness with constraint and eagerness with dishonest gain. First Timothy 3:6 reminds us that a leader in the church should not be "a novice, lest being puffed up with pride he fall into the same condemnation as the devil." Too often Christians are seized by a zeal for exposing error and launch into full-blown discernment ministries without either learning and apprenticing from others more experienced, or even checking out their findings with others. As Proverbs 11:14 and 15:22 show us, the general principle is that wisdom and safety occur in a multitude of counselors. They may not always be right, and we may sometimes have to strike out on our own; but we should seriously and critically examine ourselves, our motives, and our conclusions whenever we find ourselves differing with all of the older, respected authorities in the field.

Lone Rangers

Constance Cumbey rose to popularity as a New Age researcher in 1982 without any measure of overt interaction with established cult apologetic ministries that had already been tracking New Age ideas for years, like Dr. Walter Martin's Christian Research Institute, the Spiritual Counterfeits Project in Berkeley, and Dr. James Bjornstadt's Institute for Contemporary Christianity.

We are not saying that the "old school" is always right or that it should be idolized. But any ideas which are radically divergent from the norm should be checked very carefully. Even Martin Luther struggled within the Roman Catholic Church for as long as he could before he became one of the "lights on a hill" of the Reformation.

But Cumbey's methodology and conclusions were not endorsed by any other apologetic organization. *Christianity Today* noted, "Cumbey has not won the full endorsement of a single respected Christian scholar or cult-watching organization."[10]

The few times Cumbey has interacted with or referred to other counter-cult ministries, it has been in criticism, accusation, or actual (perhaps unwitting) misrepresentation of the ministry's position or action. In correspondence with Elliot Miller (Christian Research Institute), author of *A Crash Course on the New Age* and acknowledged by many as one of the leading evangelical experts on New Age thought, Cumbey answered Miller's professional courtesy request for exchange of materials with:

> You state that I have to furnish you certain things. I feel I do not have to do any such thing—unless directed by the Lord.
>
> I feel further that you should examine your own heart and mind in regards to the following:
> a. Why you did not bring this material out yourself.
> b. What bias you still have in favor of the New Age Movement.
> As for me, I was never involved in the New Age Movement.[11]

Cumbey also dismisses the Spiritual Counterfeits Project (SCP) in spite of its vast contributions to the evangelical evaluation and response to the New Age Movement.[12] In one of her charges against SCP researcher and cofounder Brooks Alexander, she says:

> Ironically, Brooks [sic] has been in the vanguard of those writing sneering articles about my work. One of the charges Brooke levelled at me was that I used occult books for sources, including *The Aquarian Conspiracy*. This is true. Every researcher on cults, including Brooke, does likewise, as Brooke very well knows. But there is an important distinction between the use I make of them and the use Brooke, in this hopefully isolated case, made of them. I quoted books such as *The Aquarian Conspiracy* solely to expose their content. Brooke actually used them for sources. Hopefully, this was due to a gap in his knowledge of the New Age Movement.[13]

Cumbey accused Alexander of not only "sneering" at her but of funneling New Age material to unsuspecting readers by quoting it approvingly. The quote above occurs in the larger context of her reference to a place where Alexander quoted a definition of *shamanism* from foremost authority on shamanism Mircea Eliade, chairman of the department of History of Religions at the University of Chicago. Cumbey is convinced that Eliade is a New Ager. She assumes that to quote from him about shamanism without discrediting him with a New Age label is, in effect, promoting New Ageism. The fact of the matter is that Eliade is a recognized authority in the field and has done more background, library, and field research into shamanism than almost anyone else. He is referred to in the *Encyclopaedia Britannica* and, New Ager or not, is an authority to be at least acknowledged and reckoned with when one discusses definitions of shamanism. Cumbey's charge against Alexander is simply unfounded.

Second, Cumbey is unfair to criticize SCP references to her as "sneering." We have reviewed the SCP articles on the New Age Movement regarding Cumbey. Nowhere did we perceive the bitterness of which they are accused. Their attitude has remained constant and kind over the years. In fact, in *The New Age Rage,* published after Cumbey's book quoted above, SCP does criticize some of Cumbey's conclusions and research methods. However, it also conscientiously notes her positive contributions too:

> On the positive side, Cumbey has effectively drawn attention to a phenomenon that deserves attention . . . . In addition, her picture of the movement's organizational network appears to be accurate and well-documented. In this respect, her work is performing a real service by raising the issue so loudly that it must be heard.[14]

Credibility

When one unwittingly falls into using witch hunting techniques such as ignoring or failing to account reasonably for the discrepancies between one's own conclusions and everyone else's, then one's credibility begins to suffer. The resultant lack of respect from other authorities for one's conclusions is often then misunderstood as unwarranted discrimination based on the unpopular position rather than on the more reasonable possibility that one's conclusions are not valid.

Constance Cumbey seems unable to see that the validity of her conclusions is being questioned not because they are unpopular, but because she has not demonstrated careful, comprehensive, verified research—which includes checking with others. Instead, she cries "discrimination!" For example, she believes she was discriminated against at a counter-cult ministry conference in California in 1983, and also that she was "roasted" by Gretchen Passantino and Chet Lackey on a television program, "The John Ankerberg Show."[15] She seems not to have considered the possibility that she was challenged because her views were unsubstantiated.

Ed Decker is a former Mormon and his Saints Alive (Ex-Mormons for Jesus) ministry has been the vehicle for many conversions to Christ from Mormonism. However, his writings and films have been controversial. He has been criticized repeatedly by other counter-Mormon evangelistic organizations for sensationalistic evangelism methods which are said to offend more Mormons than they attract.

Pre-eminent ex-Mormon researchers Jerald and Sandra Tanner have disparaged his highly speculative theories concerning what Decker sees as secret connections between Mormon symbolism and Satanism.[16] In the April 1988 edition of the Tanners' *Salt Lake City Messenger,* the Tanners summarized their feelings about Ed Decker's lack of credibility for some of what he teaches:

> It has been with great sorrow that we have lifted the pen to deal with these issues. We are, in fact, deeply grieved by the whole situation. Nevertheless, we sincerely believe that the type of excesses which we have pointed out in *The Lucifer-God Doctrine* can have a devastating effect on thousands of people. We have sought God's help about the matter and have concluded that strong action is necessary to prevent the spread of erroneous information that could undermine people's trust in material published on Mormonism and Christianity.[17]

What a shame that Christians working in the same mission field with the same purposes are unable to present a front against the cults that is united by common faith, responsible research, and dependable conclusions tested by reason, evidence, and wise counsel! Witch hunting characterized by a lack of cooperative testing with established Christians hurts us all. Everyone should be careful to take into account Christian views which are contrary to their own, especially when those views are held by authorities or leaders in the field.

WITCH HUNTING MISUNDERSTANDS ALTERNATE WORLDVIEWS

Perhaps as a corollary to this disassociation with other discernment ministries, witch hunting often fails to take into account even major differences among world religions and worldviews. This may be because many Christians with a real heart for evangelism are also young in the Lord and young in age. Without a solid background of study and education in biblical doctrine, it is very easy to misunderstand the teachings, backgrounds, and worldviews of world religions. It is easy to confuse Mormonism and Hinduism, thinking they have the same religious ideas simply because both believe in more than one god (polytheism) even though the way they explain and understand their respective beliefs about their gods is very different. In the same way, many people do not realize that Hinayanic Buddhism, while incorporating religious practices and traditions, is actually atheistic. Others lump Satanism and witchcraft together, failing to understand that their beliefs are as divergent from each other as are the views of the Way International cult from those of the Jehovah's Witnesses.

This harms the credibility of Christian scholarship in the non-Christian world. Failing to understand someone's beliefs and worldview also makes people think you do not care enough to find out what they really believe—you just want to ridicule them. Finally, inaccurate understanding or presentation of contrary beliefs sabotages one's apologetic against those beliefs. It is impossible to be persuasive in your refutation of a position if you cannot even articulate or properly represent that position. Jesus said he was truth incarnate (John 14:6), and the Bible commands all believers to adhere to truth (Eph. 4:25; 3 John 3,4; Acts 26:25). We cannot afford to be sloppy in our discernment and description of false belief.

For example, in *The Hidden Dangers of the Rainbow,* author Constance Cumbey confuses the Nazi doctrine of the master race with the Theosophical cult's belief in ascended masters. This fundamental error in interpretation is ably pointed out and answered in a critique by Dr. J. Gordon Melton, founder and director of the Institute for the Study of American Religion.[18]

> In the former case [Nazism], the evolved people were an entire race, the product of superior genes; as a group, they were born more evolved. In the latter case [Theosophical doctrine], specific individuals from the human species had evolved, spiritually not biologically, to a place of cosmic leadership. By associating these two ideas, Cumbey erroneously ascribes Nazi ideology to the New Age Movement. Given the present situation, living as we do in a post-Holocaust world, such ascription is more than a minor error, it is serious slander.[19]

In our desire to avoid witch hunting, we must rise to the challenge of comprehensive scholarship and avoid myopic vision that assumes our own limited, initial perspective to be unfailingly accurate and objective.

COMMITMENT TO EXCELLENCE

In this chapter we have seen several important principles we can use to evaluate our own discernment and that of others. Those we have used as examples are Christians who desire to judge accurately between orthodoxy and heresy. Unfortunately, they sometimes slip into witch hunting. This can happen to any of us but must be avoided at all costs.

When equipping ourselves for biblical judgment, we need to ensure that we have a proper understanding of the Church and its diversity; a healthy regard for other leaders (recognizing they are not always right, but they do have a mature perspective); and an accurate understanding of alternate belief systems. Consistent failure in any of these areas makes our discernment vulnerable to distortion, inaccuracy, and the negative power to both convict the innocent and excuse the guilty.

In the next two chapters we examine the areas which provide the most opportunity for faulty discernment: errors in thinking and the misuse of logic.

CHAPTER 4

Fallible "Facts"

*B*ob was a fervent agnostic before he became a Christian. He used to go to the library and research arguments against the existence of God, alleged Bible contradictions, and reasons Christianity was a myth. During the early parts of the Jesus Movement when hippie Christians went down to the Southern California beaches to witness, Bob would be there too, following them across the sand, arguing with them about how foolish it was to be a Christian.

Then Bob became a Christian. At the moment the Holy Spirit touched him and he surrendered his life to the Lord, he thought, "All of this intellectual game playing doesn't mean anything. Jesus Christ is who he said he was and I have to follow him." His Christianity became as radical as his agnosticism had been before. He thirsted after Bible knowledge, jumped into studying theology and doctrine, and gave more intellectually to Christianity than he ever had to agnosticism.

But he started running into problems. He didn't

understand how certain verses that appeared contradictory fit together. He had complicated questions about the doctrine of the Trinity, free will and sovereignty, and creation. He couldn't become an instant scholar overnight, so he started asking his pastors and Bible study teachers questions. He was startled when they didn't come up with satisfying answers. Instead, they doubted his sincerity, accused him of doubting God, and told him that he should just practice trusting God. Bob wasn't satisfied, but he certainly didn't want to offend God or lose faith, so he gave up trying to use his mind in Christianity. He even stopped reading his Bible because every time he did, he came up with more questions and there was nobody to answer them for him.

Providentially, Bob didn't stay in the abyss of anti-intellectualism. He figured out that if Jesus were really *the truth* then Christians didn't have to be afraid of truth. And if part of being created in the image of God and being redeemed by Jesus meant being able to worship and serve with his *mind* as well as his heart and strength (Deut. 6:5; Matt. 22:37), then he *could* think about Christianity. Thinking does not equal doubting, questioning does not equal lack of faith, and studying does not equal failure to trust the Holy Spirit. That was the beginning of our ministry.

Unfortunately, many Christians continue to think the way Bob first did because they have not learned basic principles of thinking, analysis, reading, and arguing by which truth can be understood and that which is false can be rejected. This lack of foundational training makes two kinds of Christians: (1) those who do not think at all and consequently do not worship and serve God with their minds; and (2) those who attempt to use their minds but end up making mistakes that could be avoided by learning how to think straight.

In fact, mistakes in thinking and reasoning make up the largest group of discernment faults. If an argument or accusation cannot stand the test of logic, is inconsistent, and fails to prove its point, it loses all rational force. However, such faulty arguments can still be dangerous emotional weapons that wrongly assassinate characters and label as heresy what is merely uncommon. These problems become even more pronounced and have even greater consequences when they are picked up by novice readers or listeners and used in ways even the mistaken witch hunter never intended.

WISDOM IS KNOWLEDGE DIRECTED BY UNDERSTANDING

The Bible uses the word *wisdom* in a variety of ways and gives it several nuances of meaning, most of which fall within the general definition of "knowledge directed by understanding." Proverbs 5:1–2 admonishes, "pay attention to my wisdom; lend your ear to my understanding, that you may preserve discretion, and that your lips may keep knowledge." Over and over the Bible links wisdom to discretion or the ability to discern properly.

We are not elevating wisdom above God, or binding God and his revelation to manmade thinking. On the contrary, wisdom cannot save us (1 Cor. 1:19–21), and without God it is worthless (Jer. 8:9), having been corrupted through the fall. However, thinking is the primary tool for all of us in our relationship with God, other Christians, and the world. Thinking permeates our conversation, our reflection, our study, our reading, our understanding, our prayer, our speaking, and our writing.

Problems in thinking occur in all of these areas with great regularity. However, God has given us reason and logic as part of the way in which we are created in his image. Reason is the mental process which underlies our beliefs, commitments, and actions. According to the Bible, reason makes men sane (Dan. 4:36), prepares one for salvation (Isa. 1:18), and reveals one's sinfulness to himself (Mark 11:31–33). Reason submitted to the authority of God and his Word is an essential foundation to Christian maturity. Logic is the use and understanding of the order and consistency with which God created the world. Using logic correctly enhances our trust in God rather than undermining it. We can and should order our thoughts according to the order God has ordained in this universe. In Isaiah 1:18 God calls us to reason concerning salvation. The whole field of apologetics presupposes a reasonable defense of our faith (1 Pet. 3:15). The apostle Paul was a champion of reasonable apologetics:

> Then Paul, as his custom was, went in to them, and for three Sabbaths reasoned with them from the Scriptures, explaining and demonstrating that the Christ had to suffer and rise again from the dead, and saying, "This Jesus whom I preach to you is the Christ" (Acts 17:2–3).

The apostle Peter understood the rational distinctives between Christianity and every other religion. Christianity is reasonable, historically verifiable, and tells the truth about reality:

> For we did not follow cunningly devised fables when we made known to you the power and coming of our

Lord Jesus Christ, but were eyewitnesses of His majesty (2 Peter 1:16).

In the same way, Christians today need to be reasonable and logical in their presentation and defense of Christianity. We do not have to make excuses for being Christians; we do not have to act as though we believe faith is unreasonable. Indeed, we are to use the reasoning ability God has given us to provide a proper vehicle for the life-transforming message of the gospel. In the following pages of this chapter, we will look at some of the most common thinking problems that contribute to witch hunting.

ASSOCIATION DOES NOT PROVE GUILT

Many of us unwittingly slip into the faulty thinking of "guilt by association." This is the idea that because someone or something is associated with something bad (or good), that someone or something must also be bad (or good). Advertising frequently appeals to this method: Drink the most popular soft drink, and you'll begin to look like California surfers and have dozens of beautiful girls chasing you. After all, the guy in the commercial is like that, and he drinks the stuff!

Sometimes a New Age researcher will look for any kind of association between those who claim to be the good guys and the bad guys in an attempt to ferret out the New Age secret agents among us. Constance Cumbey, in a talk at a Houston prophecy conference, used this method to "prove" that counter-cult organization Spiritual Counterfeits Project could be a secret New Age organization. How did she know? One reason she gave was that their book, *New Age Rage,* was published by Revell. Well, Revell also publishes New Age books—there's the connection! Revell publishes New Age books, Revell publishes SCP books; therefore, the SCP book must also be New Age. This is a blatant example of guilt by association. That is, declaring one guilty of a particular offense because of the company he keeps. If guilt by association were a valid logical method, then we could assume that if Revell published a Bible, the Bible somehow could be legitimately labeled New Age.

A critic complained to our previous radio station about our program, "Psychology: Friend or Foe?" We had as our guest Martin Bobgan, author of *Psycho Heresy,* representing the position that all psychotherapy is evil and unbiblical. Our other guests were Dr. John Carter and Dr. Keith Edwards from the Rosemead Graduate School of Psychology (at Biola University), representing the position that some principles and techniques from psychology can be used successfully to help someone if they do not conflict with biblical principles.

Our critic decided that this was not an issue to be debated in a public arena. He wanted us to reject dogmatically anything remotely tainted with psychology and not give our audience a chance to judge for themselves. Rather than dealing with the specific principles, examples, and verses Dr. Carter and Dr. Edwards used, our critic dismissed them entirely by writing:

> Ninety-nine percent of clinical so-called christian [sic] psychologists use some Freudian and Jungian theory in dealing with past hurts. Freud was a God hating atheist and Jung was involved in spiritism and admits communicating with spirits in his later years. Yet Carter quoted these men as part of "God's truth outside the Bible."[1]

On the contrary, Carter did not quote "these men" as part of God's truth, but particular principles from these men. Carter not only criticized many aspects of psychology, including Jung and Freud, he also repeatedly affirmed that any *details* of God's truth outside the Bible *must* conform to revealed biblical principles. For example, the Bible does not state that a mule, the offspring of union between a horse and a donkey, is sterile. But the Bible does record that God created life on earth to reproduce after its own kind (Gen. 1:12,21–25). It has given us the *principle* of species integrity which is then *detailed* outside the Bible.

Our critic condemned Carter unfairly by associating him with psychologists he characterized as anti-Christian. His reasoning went like this. Carter is a psychologist. Freud and Jung were pioneering psychologists. Freud was an atheist. Jung was an occultist. Therefore, Carter must be an atheist and/or an occultist—or at least overwhelmingly influenced by such thinking!

One may disagree with Carter and Edwards that psychological principles and biblical truth can be integrated, but that is a completely different discussion. Regardless of one's attitudes toward the many real problems in contemporary psychology, it is not right to condemn any Christian psychologist by using guilt by association.

A DEFINITION BIG ENOUGH TO SINK A BATTLESHIP

One of the most prevalent faulty techniques of persuasion used both in the world and, unfortunately, all too frequently in the Church, is that of expanding one's definition or making it so vague that it can cover anything. If your definition is broad enough or vague enough, you can use it to indict or approve at your whim.

Definitions that are too broad begin including within their boundaries things that do not really belong. If we say that horses are animals with four feet that pull wagons, we are too broad. Does that take into consideration oxen? Mules? Reindeer?

How about advertising a general analgesic/decongestant by saying, "for that achy-painy-stuffy feeling"? You could probably interpret that to cover many physical symptoms from which you suffer periodically, and end up using more and spending more for this over-the-counter drug than is really necessary or even therapeutic.

Vague definitions are just as versatile. A granola bar can be labeled "all natural ingredients" to persuade you it is healthy for you, when the ingredient list (in small print, of course) shows you that the main "natural" ingredient is refined sugar!

Cultists are adept at vague definitions. The Mormons, for example, are taught to believe in the "miraculous" birth of Jesus Christ. That sounds a lot like the biblical virgin birth, but it's not. Instead, Mormons are taught (with vague terminology again) that God the Father, who has a glorified body, came down to earth and had intercourse with Mary to produce Jesus Christ.

A unique use of the broad or vague definition is to not define one's terms at all. Whole books have been written on subjects which have never been defined within the book. We reviewed a book on apologetics that defined the best apologetics system as "veridicalism." The book contains examples of veridicalism and defined some of its limits, but we finished the book still wondering what this position meant. By tracing the root of the word in the *Oxford-English Dictionary,* we discovered that it meant, roughly, "truthism." We would never disagree that the best apologetics is the truth system, but we might disagree about whether or not this author had a proper understanding of the truth system, even if he did dress it up in the fancy terminology of *veridicalism.*

Unfortunately, Christians often slip into using broad or vague definitions that do not communicate concisely or accurately but, in fact, confuse and distort. As Christians we should be sure that we define not only terms with which our audience might not be familiar but also terms which we use differently than do most people.

Dave Hunt gave a much too broad definition of *sorcery* in his *The Seduction of Christianity* and then used that broad definition in a variety of ways throughout the book. It is not just that broad definitions are cumbersome; they are misleading and do not teach readers to discern accurately.

This is how Hunt defined *sorcery:*

> One word that is often used to encompass all pagan/occult practices is "sorcery." In the following pages, when we use that word our intended meaning will be: any attempt to manipulate reality (internal, external, past, present, or future) by various mind-over-matter techniques that run the gamut from alchemy and astrology to positive/possibility thinking.[2]

This definition is so broad that Christians and even the Lord himself could be sorcerers! God is spirit (John 4:24) and his mind certainly has mastery over the material world. Is he a sorcerer? Scripture commands Christians to pray, using their minds and spirits to participate in God's intervention in the world. Is prayer sorcery?

These are two obvious examples that we can readily see should be exempted from this broad definition. But using a critical definition broad enough to capture friend and foe alike runs the very real risk of capturing as foes some who are actually friends but who do not stand out as easily from sorcery as, for example, God does.

We used the preceding example in a review of *Seduction,* to which Hunt replied,

> You find fault with our "definition of sorcery." In fact we do not define sorcery, but explain the specific meaning we adopt for our purposes, which is certainly a legitimate method used in logic. . . . [You called] it a "definition of sorcery" which it was neither intended nor stated to be. This is a misrepresentation of what we wrote. Is this deliberate, or [are the Passantinos] the one[s] who need the "logic lesson"?[3]

This represents another problem any of us could fall into by reacting defensively when we are criticized. When the definition is challenged, rename it and go on. *Cornerstone* replied to Hunt's letter at length, noting the following concerning his "meaning" of sorcery:

> Your paragraph denying that *Seduction* gives a definition of sorcery is a prime example of the difficulties we have with your book. . . . To give a specific meaning for a word is to define the word. Bob [Passantino] didn't say that you claimed your definition was final or that it was accurate biblically or historically. . . .
>
> We're concerned because the meaning you attributed to "sorcery" has now been conveyed to thousands of people who have read your book. If your definition/meaning is to have any usefulness to your readership, it must be able to stand in the marketplace. . . .

> If your definition is only good for the purposes of the book, then how is the average reader to use it for his own purposes in discernment? We feel that if you (or the next guy) are going to charge people with sorcery, witchcraft, black magic, or occultism, then the standard definitions for those terms ought to be adopted.[4]

Another way of manipulating definitions is to borrow a term or phrase from someone else, give it your own definition, and then refute that "straw man" definition. Dennis Fulton is a fiery young evangelist in southern California. His fervency and zeal for the Lord shine clearly in his publications through the Believers Fellowship *Proclaimer.* But he slips into witch hunting in his essay on "The Abomination of Psychology" when he switches term definitions under the heading "Is All Truth God's Truth?"

Most Christians who use the phrase "all truth is God's truth" use it as an affirmation of God's omniscience: nothing that is really true escapes God's apprehension of it as truth (Ps. 31:5). The Christian who serves Jesus as the Truth (John 14:6) need not fear science, history, archaeology, philosophy, ethics, or any other pursuit of truth in any area of existence. What is actually true is under the authority of God and cannot possibly contradict him or his Word. There are many things the world *calls* true that are not true. Evolution is not *true;* it is a theory predicated on the unproved supposition that all life developed spontaneously from non-life, without personal direction or design from a Creator. The *facts* of life should never be confused with the *theories* men advance to try to explain the facts.

Fulton makes this confusion. He chastises Christians who would dare believe such a phrase, saying:

One must seriously answer this question, seeing as it has allowed the teachings of men like Jung, Skinner, Adler, Rogers and Maslow, to prepare the next generation of "Christian" counselors, educators, and, God forbid, even pastors! Is *all* truth God's truth? This is really the psychologist's way of saying that even if Carl Rogers or Carl Jung happened to stumble onto something that works, then it must be God's own truth! "Truth" being what "appears" to work (frighteningly most of it does not)![5]

No responsible Christian who uses the phrase "all truth is God's truth" means that truth is determined by whatever works. It is true that truth works, but not everything that works is truth. For example, you can open a door by blowing it up or turning the knob. Both ways work, but only turning the knob is the right way for it to work. *Utilitarianism* is completely contrary to the absolutism of Scripture. By switching definitions, Fulton has stuffed his own straw man and then knocked it down. He has done nothing to criticize the actual view represented by the phrase.

Sloppy definitions help no one. They do not provide an accurate yardstick for discerning between truth and error. By their very sloppiness they can be manipulated to free the guilty and snare the innocent.

APPEAL TO INAPPROPRIATE AUTHORITY

Most of us have a weakness when it comes to authority. We tend to appeal to authority when we need it to back us up, and we are intimidated by it when it is used against us. Citing or calling on the power of an inappropriate authority to buttress our case is a very persuasive technique. Sadly, even Christians sometimes use this invalid way to win an argument.

More simply put, appealing to inappropriate authority assumes that truth gets truer if someone important says it, even if that important person has no particular knowledge of that field. On the contrary, two plus two still equals four, no matter if a mathematician, God, a zoologist, or our five-year-old son says it. Conversely, the popular proposition, "People can achieve anything they want" is not true whether Shirley MacLaine, Ronald Reagan, or even Mother Theresa says it.

Dave Hunt[6] and Martin and Deidre Bobgan[7] appeal to authority by quoting Nobel prize winner Richard Feynman criticizing psychoanalysis. Hunt notes, "Nobel prize winner Richard Feynman says that 'psychoanalysis is not a science'."[8] The Bobgans state, "Nobelist Richard Feynman, in considering the scientific status of psychotherapy, says that 'psychoanalysis is not a science,' and that it is 'perhaps even more like witch doctoring'."[9]

Before we look at the various thinking problems presented here, we need to note that our criticism of Hunt and the Bobgans does not mean that we endorse all forms of psychotherapy. Psychotherapy has its own problems which we will not address here but which are better answered by examining its foundations and conclusions than by appealing to the opinions of someone outside the field.[10]

Richard Feynman was a brilliant atomic physicist who worked in pioneering atomic energy and weaponry. His Nobel prize was awarded for his work in physics. He was an inspiring scientist, teacher, and innovative researcher. His ability to think creatively in the field of quantum electrodynamics was unsurpassed.

But he was not an expert in psychology, psychotherapy, or the philosophy of science. He was opinionated. And he cared little for subjects which did not interest him.

In his autobiography *Surely You're Joking, Mr. Feynman* he said concerning a philosophy seminar he attended: "And, just like it should in all stories about philosophers, it ended up in complete chaos."[11] But there are hundreds of professional philosophers, including Christian philosophers, who would disagree with Feynman's caricature of philosophy. He is entitled to his opinion, but his opinion is not substantiated by experts in the field or by the evidence.

Martin Bobgan stated on our Answers In Action radio program that Feynman's opinion was credible because he was a scientist stating that psychoanalysis was not scientific—his expertise was in science. However, Feynman was a physics scientist, not a scientific philosopher or historian, or even a specialist in the theory of science and science education. And even if he were, he has presented no working familiarity with psychoanalysis by which his judgment can be considered definitive. He won the Nobel prize in physics for his atomic research, not for his definition prowess.

If Hunt and the Bobgans wish to appeal to Feynman's opinions as authoritative because of his general knowledge or because he must be smart to get a Nobel prize, then why not accept Feynman's other opinions? What did he think about God and religion?

Several years ago Feynman attended a costume party at the Jet Propulsion Laboratory in Pasadena. The party invitation read, "Come dressed as a character from myth or legend." Here's how *Los Angeles Times* columnist Jack Smith reported it:

> "That's Feynman over there," my wife told me. "He's Moses."
> Feynman was in a pure white cotton robe and wore a long gray beard.
> I walked over to introduce myself. "You're Feynman," I said.
> He shook his head: "I'm God."
> Later I told [host Al] Hibbs: "Feynman's God."
> He nodded. "We've known that all along," he said.[12]

Would you respect his opinion about God, his favorite "character from myth or legend"? But there's more. Feynman was interviewed on public television's *Nova* concerning his views on religion:

> I think it's much more interesting to live not knowing than to have answers which might be wrong. I have approximate answers and possible beliefs and different degrees of certainty about different things.

> But I'm not absolutely sure of anything and there are many things I don't know anything about, such as whether it means anything to ask why we're here, and what the question might mean. I might think about it a little bit and if I can't figure it out, then I go on to something else. But I don't have to know an answer.

> I don't feel frightened by not knowing things, by being lost in a mysterious universe without having any purpose, which is the way it really is, as far as I can tell possibly.

> It doesn't frighten me.[13]

By committing the fallacy of appealing to inappropriate authority, Hunt and Bobgan have elevated Feynman to an unwarranted position of authority concerning psychology because he agrees with them. But they certainly wouldn't hail him as an authority concerning God or religion. Nor would they appear likely to change their views were a scientist of stature equal to Feynman to wholeheartedly endorse psychotherapy. This is not fair reporting. It leads one's audience to believe they can trust the authorities one cites, even though those authorities lack the necessary qualifications.

CONDEMNATION BY VOCABULARY OR QUOTE

This thinking problem has to do with the unreliable method of determining one's orthodoxy or heresy on the basis of his vocabulary and/or on the basis of the orthodoxy or heresy of those he quotes. This could be considered a subgroup of the guilt-by-association fallacy, specializing in declaring one's guilt on the basis of his word choice and citations.

It is true that one can often tell an author's basic perspective by looking at the spectrum of sources he has consulted. It is also true that select groups often adopt specialized vocabularies to describe their ideas or to explain themselves to others.

However, vocabulary and quotes must be analyzed in context before one can be justified in appealing to them to support a charge of heresy or vindication.

At least as important as the "who" of citations is the "why" of citations. The Bible quotes Satan, but the "why" is to reveal Satan's wickedness and lying nature (John 8:44). The Bible does not quote Satan approvingly. When a biblical discerner criticizes someone for citing heretics without carefully noting and reporting *why* those heretics were quoted, he is misleading his audience and condemning his target without proper evidence.

The apostle Paul quotes Greek philosophers and poets in various places, including Acts 17. These philosophers were pagans and, of course, did not believe in the true God. Does Paul say he agrees with all they said? No, he cites them because they share a common belief, namely, that existence comes from deity. All of us are "offspring of God" by creation, even though we must be redeemed by Jesus' death on the cross to be children of God by adoption (John 1:12; Rom. 8:14–17; 10:9–10).

Sometimes people are unfairly chastised for quoting or referring to non-Christian or heretical sources and teachers either approvingly or without warning their audiences that these sources and teachers are poison.

Teachers do have a responsibility to give their audiences sufficient information for responsible discernment. But just as Paul did not have to justify himself in Acts 17 for his quotations of pagans, Christian leaders do not always have to assume complete gullibility on the part of their audience nor invincible satanic power on the part of the sources they quote.

Dave Hunt criticized two Campus Crusade for Christ writers, Stephen Douglass and Lee Roddy, for their quotations of occultist Napoleon Hill:

> Yet they recommend him [Napoleon Hill] and his books highly, which contain occultism that they apparently overlooked, and which could seduce those who, upon endorsement, read Hill's books for themselves.[14]

Hunt himself noted that Douglass and Roddy cautioned readers about some of Hill's problems, but he still used them as a prime example of how open advocacy of sorcery has slipped into the Christian Church because of unwitting dupes like Douglass and Roddy (who, since the first edition of *Seduction,* have removed references to Hill from their own book).

Is Hunt right? Were Douglass and Roddy dupes of the New Age Movement, or were they quoting like the apostle Paul did? Here is *Cornerstone* magazine's opinion:

> A major point of *Seduction* is that people like Douglass and Roddy . . . are bringing "a mixture of truth and error" into the Church. . . . Your [Hunt's] point is that they are contributing to the apostasy of the Church—unwittingly, perhaps, but bringing in poison nonetheless.
>
> . . . Douglass and Roddy [go] into detail about Bible study, the plan of salvation, the sinner's prayer, and being filled with the Holy Spirit. . . . Does their silence about Hill's occultism necessarily indicate oversight or ignorance of it?. . . . Must Christian authors always add a warning when they cite a New Age teacher as a source of their information?
>
> I don't know. At the present, I feel the answer is "most of the time, yes; but no, not always"—the frequency would depend on the audience and the contents of the rest of the book.[15]

A counterexample to this unfortunate mistake of condemnation by quotation can be made by misusing the footnotes for Dave Hunt's or Constance Cumbey's books. They quote frequently and at length from New Age sources. They are quoting in *criticism* of the New Agers. However, with the pattern of witch hunting fallacies that too many Christians have today, Hunt and Cumbey could be condemned right along with Douglass and Roddy!

In *Seduction* Hunt quotes from C. S. Lewis once, approvingly. In *Beyond Seduction*[16] he quoted from Lewis twelve times, all approvingly. He quoted from Lewis without reservation seven times in *Whatever Happened to Heaven?*[17]

We believe that Lewis was one of the greatest Christian minds of this century, and his faith was deep and healthy. But he also accepted a form of theistic evolution and had problems with biblical inerrancy. He even stated,

> If we let Him—for we can prevent Him, if we choose—He will make the feeblest and filthiest of us into a god or goddess, dazzling, radiant, immortal creature, pulsating through with such energy and joy and wisdom and love as we cannot now imagine, a bright stainless mirror which reflects back to God perfectly (although, of course, on a smaller scale) His own boundless power and delight and goodness. The process will be long and in parts very painful; but that is what we are in for. Nothing less. He meant what He said.[18]

By applying witch hunting techniques to Lewis's vocabulary, we can declare him a New Age or Mormon heretic. This could be done in spite of the fact that the larger context of his argument is drawn from an orthodox interpretation of 2 Peter 1:4.

By using condemnation by quotation techniques, we could even declare Hunt a dupe of the New Age Movement for quoting other Lewis material approvingly. One danger of using inadequate tests is that they might also ensnare you!

There was a computer study done several years ago to determine "scientifically" if Paul had written the New Testament epistles traditionally ascribed to him. By tabulating the word frequency (the number of times certain words are used in similar text lengths) of the epistles the programmers already accepted as Pauline, they believed they could then use those figures to analyze the other letters to ascertain their Pauline authenticity. This scientific computer analysis "proved" that Paul was not the author of most of the books usually ascribed to him.

But the programmers had forgotten to consider the subject matter of the different passages and their dates of composition. Both of these factors adequately explained the discrepancies; had they been included in the study, they would have vindicated the Pauline authorship. These critics wrongly assumed that vocabulary or word usage patterns could be predicted without considering any outside influences and used to determine the authorship of a work.[19]

Witch hunting often slips into bad word counting in an effort to ferret out New Agers and heretics. Constance Cumbey, in *Hidden Dangers of the Rainbow*,[20] uses this to show that Christian writer Tom Sine is being used (knowingly or not) to promote the New Age Movement plan: "He uses the phrase 'New Age' itself approximately 150 times in his book, more than even Marilyn Ferguson in *The Aquarian Conspiracy*."[21] But by itself, that vocabulary use of "New Age" means nothing about Tom Sine's orthodoxy or heresy. Why did he use the phrase that much? Was he approving it, criticizing it, or using the phrase in his own way to signify a concept which is not the New Age Movement as we know it? Perhaps he is using it for a biblical concept for which he has picked an inappropriate symbolic name? Cumbey does not tell us. The simple repetition of the phrase is apparently sufficient evidence to warrant her condemnation. Cumbey would not appreciate being insinuated as a dupe of the New Age Movement because she uses "New Age" in *Hidden Dangers* many more times than did Sine in his book!

Condemnation by vocabulary is poor argumentation and totally inadequate for accurately identifying orthodoxy and heterodoxy.

THINKING STRAIGHT

Although we cite some authors' works more than others for examples of witch hunting, we are not dismissing all value from their work nor personally attacking them. Any of us, professional cult critics or lay people, are vulnerable both to using witch hunting techniques and to falling for their persuasive power. But these weaknesses should prompt us to be ever-vigilant to maintain the highest standards of criticism or endorsement.

In this chapter we have examined four common errors in thinking which can sabotage biblical discernment.

Guilt by association is an easy problem into which we can fall. Because two parties have similar likes, beliefs, habits, or activities, we tend to believe that commonality in that area proves similarity in other areas. But it doesn't.

Broad and vague definitions give us no ability to measure and understand concepts accurately. Such definitions cover too much or do not provide us with clear enough limits to distinguish them from other concepts.

Appeal to inappropriate authority is an easy argument to use. Many people find it intimidating to criticize any kind of authority figure. However, truth does not get truer just because somebody important or famous says it.

Finally, *condemnation by vocabulary or quote* is deceptively convincing. All you have to do is compare terminology and count instances of word usage. But this is just busy work. It tells you nothing about how the vocabulary is used or why a particular work or author is cited.

In order to protect yourself from heresy and embrace orthodoxy, you must follow clear, cohesive, and consistent guidelines with workable tools of biblical understanding. God does not need us to indulge in easy arguments which do not really prove their cases in the effort to defend Christian truth.

In the next chapter we will examine some of the most commonly used logical errors of witch hunting. Far from being just an academic exercise in logic, this chapter will show major pitfalls of witch hunting and provide sound alternate principles for biblical apologetics.

CHAPTER 5

Reason Abuse

*T*here is a game called *Propaganda* that teaches players "to learn the fascinating techniques used by professionals to influence public opinion."[1] Christians should have thought of that game! Scripture consistently admonishes us to test everything (1 Thess. 5:21–22). The Bible exhorts us to be mature in our relationship to the Lord, no longer falling for the craftiness of the world:

> That we should no longer be children, tossed to and fro and carried about with every wind of doctrine, by the trickery of men, in the cunning craftiness by which they lie in wait to deceive, but, speaking the truth in love, may grow up in all things into Him who is the head—Christ (Eph. 4:14–15).

Propaganda teaches players to recognize and respond to crafty political speeches, enticing sales pitches, and glitzy advertising. In short, it teaches players to think logically, to recognize logical fallacies, and to avoid promoting or believing propaganda.

We cannot afford to accept or promote propaganda. Christians who have a burden for defending the faith (1 Pet. 3:15) have a responsibility to ensure that their arguments are reasonable, truthful, and logical. By studying the following four witch hunting logical pitfalls, you will not only protect yourself from falling for these errors, you will also learn how to evaluate beliefs with scriptural, logical principles.

DON'T SAW THE LIMB
YOU'RE SITTING ON

One of the most common logical errors is *self-refutation*—an argument or statement that refutes itself; one that, in its very assertion, denies its own claim. For example, it is absurd to say, "there is no truth." In the very act of asserting "there is no truth," an alleged truth is being asserted, namely, that there is no truth. But if that is a valid truth, then it must be false! "You're wrong if you judge" is itself a judgment, which, if accurate, incriminates itself. Self-refuting statements get us nowhere. They are as supportive to our position as sitting on a limb in order to saw it off the tree—we end up falling to the ground.

Christian apologist J. P. Moreland explains self-refutation this way:

> When a statement fails to satisfy itself (i.e., to conform to its own criteria of validity or acceptability), it is self-refuting. Such statements are necessarily false. The facts which falsify them are unavoidably given with the statement when it is uttered.

> Consider some examples. "I cannot say a word of English" is self-refuting when uttered in English. "I do not exist" is self-refuting, for one must exist to utter

it. The claim "there are no truths" is self-refuting. If it is false, then it is false. But if it is true, then it is false as well, for in that case there would be no truths, including the statement itself.[2]

Self-refuting arguments can come packaged in single self-stultifying statements (like those discussed above) or in broader arguments that self-contradict.

Witch hunting often falls into similar traps. One interesting example is found in Constance Cumbey's *Hidden Dangers*. Briefly, Cumbey describes how the New Age conspiracy (which she believes is the antichrist religion prophesied in 1 Thess. 5 and 2 Thess. 2) was maintained over the years.

First, she states in several places that "The Plan" was hidden from the outside world (and especially Christians) partly through the use of "blinds" and secret codes, both before and after the key agenda year, 1975:

Work was to remain low-profile until 1975—when the hitherto secret teachings about the "New Age Christ" and "Heirarchy" could be publicly disseminated by all available media.[3]

After the secrecy order came down, the Society began to communicate by secret signs and words of recognition. This practice continues today within the modern New Age Movement. It is specifically designed to keep information from hostile investigators.[4]

Second, Cumbey states in several places that The Plan was *not* hidden by blinds and secret codes, either before or after 1975:

These [hitherto secret teachings] omitted little or nothing. They ranged from the attitude of the Hierarchy toward Jews (negative) through dietary advice. Step by step they plotted the coming "New Age," with instructions for the institution of the necessary New World Order through the use of identifying rainbows. . . . all were covered extensively in the Alice Bailey writings. . . .

Comparing the Bailey teachings with the state of the Movement and its constituent organizations, it is clear that her instructions have been followed meticulously.[5]

The Movement was to keep a low profile until 1975. Then it had permission to take everything public—including the fact and nature of "The Plan" itself. Everything hidden was to be revealed and there was to be a no-holds-barred propaganda drive after that time, spreading the previously esoteric teachings of the New Age along with the anticipation of a New Age Christ by every media vehicle available. However, even before 1975, the stage had been carefully set.[6]

Third, Cumbey asserts that she was able to understand The Plan because, using her training as an attorney, she took the plainest meaning available that fit the facts.[7] But she says in another place that Christians can break The Plan's "secret codes" because they have the supernatural aid of God:

[Bailey] discounted the possibility that the Movement might be embarrassed by these books falling into the wrong hands. Alice was confident that they would be incomprehensible to anyone but an initiate.

Had she been more familiar with the Scriptures, she would have realized the folly of this position:

> Many shall be purified, and made white, and
> tried; but the wicked shall do wickedly: and none
> of the wicked shall understand; but the wise
> shall understand (Daniel 12:10 KJV).

Comparing the Bailey teachings with the state of the
Movement and its constituent organizations, it is
clear that her instructions have been followed meticulously.[8]

Here's where the limb-sawing comes in. Referring
back to the above quotes, try to answer the following
questions for Cumbey:

1. Was The Plan secret before 1975? If so, how
   then can Cumbey challenge anyone to compare
   the literature (written before 1975) with the
   Movement to confirm that the Movement follows The Plan?
2. Was The Plan brought into the open after 1975?
   If so, then why does Cumbey also assert that
   the blinds and codes are still used today?
3. How does Cumbey test what is a "blind" and
   what is really part of The Plan? Is it by plain
   sense of the passage (p. 34), or only by supernatural discernment (pp. 50 and 114)?
4. If Cumbey insists on using Daniel 12:10 as her
   authority to identify New Agers as "wicked"
   and Cumbey, et.al., as "wise," then we should
   conclude from that verse that only Cumbey and
   other "wise" ones can understand The Plan.
   How, then, have New Agers been able to follow
   The Plan "meticulously" without understanding it?

This is not nitpicking. She cannot maintain mutually exclusive or contradictory stands. The Plan was
either secret or open, not both secret *and* open in the

same way at the same time. It either became open or stayed secret, but not both became secret *and* stayed open in the same way at the same time. And either Cumbey is wise and the New Agers are wicked, or Cumbey is wicked and the New Agers are wise.

Responsible scholarship and reasonable Christianity deserve better thinking than this.

SIMILAR DOES NOT PROVE SAME

Another common problem in thinking is the assumption that because two ideas have similarities, they must be the same or come from the same source. Some researchers on the New Age Movement interpret Genesis 3:5 to mean Satan promised Adam and Eve godhood. Then they point to practically any cult or religion that identifies man as deity or able to progress (evolve) into godhood and say, "That's the same lie Satan propagated in the Garden."[9]

A careful reading of the passage shows that Satan lied in telling Eve that God did not say they would die from eating the forbidden fruit. He then offered his own lying *explanation* for God's prohibition: God's moral deficiencies (perhaps jealousy) made him afraid for them to be like him *in knowing good and evil* by their own standards. God's threat was fulfilled in Genesis 3:22, where God said that Adam and Eve had become like him—in knowing good and evil.

However, even if such an interpretation of Genesis 3:5 were accurate, the other cults and religions could have come up with their own forms of deification heresy. Similar ideas about the deification of man are not necessarily *the same* ideas. Hindu ideas of man being divine come from a *pantheistic* presupposition, that is, that the universe and God are one,

111

they are identified with each other. Mormon ideas of man progressing to godhood are more like ancient Greek polytheism, that is, belief in many gods.

Another example of this type of problem comes from ex-Mormon, Ed Decker. Decker has done extensive research in Mormonism and a lesser amount in satanism. However, he approaches his comparative study of the two with the faulty assumption that if he finds something similar between the two, then he has found proof that Mormonism is satanism in disguise.

All Christians agree that the underlying inspiration of all cults, including Mormonism, is Satan, the father of lies (John 8:44). However, this does not mean that every thought of every cultist is automatically demonized, or derived from Satan.

Decker's faulty reasoning sounds very reasonable when it is presented in a sophisticated way and when it is mixed with a little bit of truth. But it really has no more validity than "seeing" a face in the clouds means Jesus is appearing in a vision, or "seeing" a woman in the stars means God determined astrological "signs" like Virgo to testify to the gospel!

Ed Decker believes that the spires atop Mormon temples and chapels are clues to the secret satanic foundation of Mormonism. He says that satanism uses a nail as a symbol of Satan's goal to "pierce" or destroy God. He thinks the spires on Mormon temples and chapels look like upside down nails, and are pointed toward the sky, beyond which is heaven, the dwelling place of God. So, these must be satanic symbols suggesting that Mormonism will destroy God. His conclusion: Mormon spires are satanic nails in disguise, proving that Mormonsim is satanic.[10]

However, Decker has produced no positive proof

that the spires of Mormonism are causally or logically identifiable with satanic nail symbolism. He also has failed to account for the literally dozens of other possible reasons and sources for the Mormon spires.

In addition to not proving one's case, such sloppy thinking also fosters bad reactions (understandably) from the very cultists we are trying to reach with the gospel. Jerald and Sandra Tanner live and minister in Salt Lake City, headquarters of the Mormon Church, and they see the effects of such sensationalistic criticisms of Mormonism. Sandra Tanner told us in an interview:

> The tone of so much of this sensationalistic literature is bad. Instead of being persuaded by Christians' love for them, Mormons who read or see this kind of literature see it as a hateful caricaturization of Mormon beliefs. It is the kind of stuff that is loaded with emotionally charged words that turn most Mormons off. If you were a Mormon, wouldn't it be hard for you to believe that I cared for you if you thought I was misrepresenting you or making fun of you?

> Christians who are into this kind of "evangelism" say you have to shock Mormons to get them to listen. But I don't think Jesus ever told us to use sensationalism, bad thinking, and offensiveness as a good pattern of evangelism.[11]

IT'S NOT ALWAYS EITHER/OR

Another problem Christians often have in discerning between good and bad is the tendency to miss some of the options. This false alternative fallacy involves thinking that something must always be "only this way" or "either this or that," never both or some other unmentioned alternative(s). It is like the salesman who says, "Will you take the blue model or the yellow model?" when you haven't yet decided to buy the item. He does not offer you the option of not buying anything at all.

Christians are responsible for maintaining the true faith, and we must guard against promoting error because of simplistic denouncements which fail to take into consideration all the options.

Here is an example to which any parent can relate. Recently we told our three children that we would take them somewhere. Unexpected company changed our plans. We explained to our children and put off our outing to another time. But we all heard loud and clear as our youngest walked out of the room declaring, "You're just mean. That's why you won't let us go. You just don't like us." In the midst of his disappointment he couldn't see any other logical possibility, such as unexepected company, that could have changed our plans.

A clear example of the false alternative fallacy is in Texe Marrs's *Dark Secrets of the New Age* and concerns his interpretation of New Testament eschatology. He describes the New Age Movement plan (actually the plan of one small New Age group, the Tara Center) to install a New Age "Christ" in a position of world leadership in 1982. Then he examines why this plan failed. Here is his analysis:

> Why was the time not ripe in 1982? Why has the New Age "Christ" failed to appear? *There can only be one explanation:* Satan has up to now been constrained by the Holy Spirit. Though Satan is surely anxious to do his dirty work, the almighty power of God has up to now denied Satan his long-awaited opportunity to seize total control. God has a timetable for these last days, known only to Him (Matt. 24:36). Neither Satan

nor any man knows when God will allow the final curtain to rise.[12]

Here is Marrs's false alternative. He assumes only one foundation: the Tara Center plan must be the Antichrist's plan. He does not allow for any other organization or time period to be the source of the Antichrist's plan. Then, based on a single alternative, he assumes that the only reason it did not work was because God restrained it for an unknown length of time.

However, if we do not affirm Marrs's assumption that this plan *must be* the Antichrist's plan, then we can see that perhaps the Tara Center plan did not work because it was not the plan prophesied in Scripture as the Antichrist's assumption of power.

Although in an ultimate sense the Holy Spirit is "in charge" of all world events, it does not necessarily follow that his direct intervention is the only possible explanation for the Tara Center plan's failure. Marrs, or any of us speculating on eschatology and world events, does our readers a disservice if he states that his own speculation is identical to biblical prophecy.

Marrs's logical problem here may not have very serious consequences in itself. However, such sloppy thinking opens the door for very dangerous consequences in other areas. If you think this way, for example, you can easily slip into thinking that anyone who disagrees with you must be in a conspiracy against you. This is the impression that Constance Cumbey gave to *Christianity Today* when they asked her about her critics: "Cumbey responds to her critics by claiming that either they have not done enough research or they themselves are a part of the conspiracy."[13]

Cumbey, or anyone who makes mistakes in thinking this way, actually sets herself up as a pope—an authority who can never be challenged or questioned. She has given you an either/or dilemma: you can be biblical and agree with her, or you can disagree and be a heretic. She fails to acknowledge that there is any possibility at all that she is wrong.

Cults often do this with their new converts. They isolate them from any means by which they could test the claims of the cult and refuse to let them know all of the options.

For example, we once had a cultist tell us that he knew his cult was true. He explained that the cult warned him that when he told his parents about the cult, they would respond to him one of two ways: they would either say he was wrong, which proved Satan was speaking through them and so the cult was right; or they would say he was right, in which case they would confirm the truthfulness of the cult. At no time did it occur to him that they might disagree, not because they were inspired by Satan, but because he really was in a cult! He fell for this false alternative fallacy and endured spiritual bondage unnecessarily.

One evening we witnessed to a cultist at the request of her brother. She was very antagonistic and at the end warned us that those who opposed "God's move" were in danger of God's judgment. She told us of other people who had opposed her group and who had died mysteriously. We were quick to point out, though, that she was making *two* false alternative fallacies. Even if we died that night on the way home, that would not vindicate her or prove that God was acting in judgment on her behalf. First, our deaths could have been unrelated to God's judgment. Second, even if God did judge us and kill us, she had

no proof that he was judging us for criticizing *her*
cult—after all, we witness to cultists from *dozens* of
different cults. How could she tell it was her god
striking us dead and not someone else's god?

But we did not die that night, and none of the
cultists therefore were tempted to claim credit for
their god's power of judgment.

THE FALSE ANALOGY

Often researchers against cults and other false belief systems fall into the trap of thinking that because two things are similar in some points, they
must be similar in all points. This is called the "false
analogy" fallacy.

A Christian talking against satanism, for example, may point to a child abuser who confessed to
being a satanist and extrapolate that satanists are
child abusers and that child abuse is a belief within
satanism.

The Christian who argues this way has not yet
proved that it was the abuser's satanism which
caused him to commit his crimes, and he has not
proved, even if that were the case, that satanism necessarily promotes child abuse.

We are not defending either satanism or child
abuse. Satanism stands diametrically opposed to
God and the Bible and everything biblical that
Christianity stands for. And Jesus declared that for
anyone who hurt a child, "It would be better for him
if a millstone were hung around his neck, and he
were thrown into the sea" (Luke 17:2). Ritualistic
abuse is the worst of both.

However, it is no more right to make a casual connection between satanism and child abuse because of
a child-abusing satanist than it would be to accuse

Christianity of promoting child abuse because a pastor of a Christian church is arrested for abusing a child. The teachings of satanism (depending on which brand you choose) are self-indulgent, and so would not necessarily forbid child abuse, while Christianity is inherently opposed to any such activity. However, to make a direct connection between satanism and child abuse requires more for evidence than a false analogy. He must show that satanism *teaches* child abuse.

Magicians Danny Korem and Andrew Kole have done a great service to Christians in exposing the fraudulent basis for much of the phenomena claimed by psychic practitioners to be supernatural or paranormal. Most of the psychic phenomena for which there is enough evidence to be conclusive can be shown to be either natural or trickery. However, when we start with the basis of biblical evidence, affirming the existence of immaterial powers (both good—angels, and bad—demons), then we must assume that some psychic phenomena could be demonic in origin.

Korem and Kole both give lip service to belief in the possibility of isolated incidents involving actual demonic power. However, both assert repeatedly the faulty analogy that if they can duplicate a phenomenon through sleight-of-hand (trickery), then they thereby have proved the true source of each report of that phenomenon.

For example, Korem discussed the pendulum, a common psychic "tool" which swings, supposedly from spiritual forces, to communicate a message from the spirit world. He explained how professional magicians use ideomotor action (uncontrollable muscular actions that are direct responses to conscious or unconscious thoughts) to duplicate many kinds of psychic phenomena, including pendulum movement. Here is his conclusion:

> The direction of movement of a pendulum, allowed to swing freely . . . is thought by some to indicate answers to questions. The movement of the pendulum, however, is simply a manifestation of ideomotor action.[14]

This same kind of conclusion appears over and over in Korem's and Kole's books: we can duplicate it naturally, so it must not be supernatural. This faulty analogy fails to take into account that even though the phenomenon can be duplicated naturally, and even though the majority of the occurrences of the phenomenon are generated naturally, that does not prove it is "simply," or in every case, generated naturally.

Perhaps the greatest danger of habitually using faulty analogies is that one runs the risks of either downplaying something too much or sensationalizing it too much. Someone who reads Korem's and Kole's books may miss their few acknowledgments of real demonic power, concentrate on their trickery explanations, and get the idea that the world of the occult is simply the world of trickery, hardly spiritually threatening. We have talked with many people who had their palms read, went to a psychic, or had their horoscopes cast because they thought they were just tricks—just games or entertainment. Then they became more and more caught up in it and experienced real demonic power and influence. As Christians who want to integrate every area of our lives with God's clear Word, we must be very careful that our explanations of supernatural phenomena do not lull people into a false complacency, a complacency that can make them vulnerable to real occultism.

On the other hand, as we have shown, it is very easy to use false analogies to sensationalize a subject. Such sensationalism can produce fear and timidity in Christians, effectively paralyzing their witness in the world for fear that they will be sucked into evil at any moment. While some forms of sensationalism seem ridiculous to most people, some people, caught up in the fervor of a sensationalist, experience very real but needless fear.

A woman called us recently asking our advice about a Christmas present for her son. He wanted a pair of cowboy boots, and the most economical pair she could find was in a major department store catalog. Unfortunately, she had been told that the stitching on the side of the boot, which showed in the catalog picture, was almost the same shape as a letter of the Greek alphabet that was the first letter in a Greek word that referred to the Antichrist. She was sincerely afraid that buying her son the cowboy boots would be taking the mark of the beast.

Funny? No, it is tragic when people's lives are ruled by fear caused by bad thinking and wrong ideas.

STRAIGHT THINKING

When we think straight, our apologetics can reflect the high biblical standards we all are trying to achieve in our ministries to defend the faith and preach the gospel. Self-discipline involves discipline of mind as well as spirit and body so we can join with the apostle Paul in saying:

For though we walk in the flesh, we do not war according to the flesh. For the weapons of our warfare are not carnal but mighty in God for pulling down strongholds, casting down arguments and every high thing that exalts itself against the knowledge of God, bringing every thought into captivity to the obedience of Christ (2 Cor. 10:3–5).

CHAPTER 6

You Could Be Next

When we or other cult watchers and researchers point out some of the sensationalism of witch hunting, this is the response we often get from other Christians: "Well, maybe that is a little bit unfair. But after all, these people they are exposing really are heretics and better to be warned too much than too little!" In the preceding three chapters we explained why witch hunting is unfair and inaccurate. The Bible clearly shows that heretics should be condemned because of their heresy, not because of faulty discernment by cult watchers. In this chapter we show that witch hunting tactics are not only unfair and unbiblical, but also that they make *all* Christians potential witch hunting targets.

CHRISTIANS OR ANTICHRIST'S PRIESTS?

Despite short disclaimers or "hate the sin, love the sinner" statements, often witch hunting rather indiscriminately accuses its targets of participating in mass delusional heresy.

For example, Dave Hunt seems to send mixed signals about Christian psychologists. On the one hand, he refers to Christian psychologists like James Dobson as "earnest Christian leaders with effective ministries."[1] He believes Dobson "sincerely desires to be biblical, [but] he has based his ministry upon a belief that was not derived from Scripture . . . ."[2] On the other hand, he also makes sweeping condemnations of all Christian psychologists—presumably including Dobson and other "earnest Christian leaders with effective ministries." The strong denouncements are perhaps most evident in Hunt's newsletters:

> "Christian psychology" represents the most deadly and at the same time the most appealing and popular form of *modernism* ever to confront the church. . . .
>
> Then what is meant by this term? What is so-called Christian psychology? It is simply one form or another of secular psychology developed by godless humanists hostile to the Bible and now dressed up in Christian language. . . .
>
> Psychotherapy is, in fact, a rival religion that cannot be integrated with Christianity. Having nothing of value to offer to anyone, much less Christians, it is both deceptive and destructive.[3]
>
> Christian psychology could almost be described as a cult inside the church. It has its own vocabulary, an endless new category of problems tagged with labels not found in the Bible and unknown to the church in its entire history. . . . In short, this cult has its own gospel, its own religious rituals administered by its own class of priests, the Christian psychologists, who have gained authority over those who only know God's Word.[4]

We agree that much of secular psychology is founded on decidedly non-Christian worldviews, and that many techniques and assumptions within secular psychology are incompatible with biblical teaching. We also agree that many "Christian psychologists," perhaps lacking a solid biblical foundation and godly wisdom, adopt many non-Christian psychological principles and ideas.

However, Dobson and some other Christian psychologists believe that they are basing their teachings on the Bible alone, and that principles from psychology are only tools or examples of principles that either are rooted in the Bible or at least are in line with and tested by biblical principles.

Disagree with them if you like, but prove your case by addressing their interpretations of Scripture, not by falsely assuming without proof that their principles couldn't have come from the Bible. This book is not the forum for a discussion of psychology and Christianity, but books which do address that issue are in the "For Further Reading" list at the back of this book.[5]

UNITY IN ESSENTIALS; DIVERSITY IN NONESSENTIALS

It is completely inappropriate for a Christian, without clear and overwhelming evidence, to label an earnest Christian leader as a cultic priest! With such flexible identifications, any Christian—even you—can be labeled a heretic.

In fact, we talked informally with Dave Hunt at the 1989 Christian Booksellers Convention in Atlanta, Georgia, and he informed us that Constance Cumbey had started accusing him of being a stooge of the New Age Movement, of being sympathetic to reconstructionism,[6] and of having his own "spirit guides."

What a contrast to the biblical pattern, which commands us to avoid accusing other Christians without ironclad proof or aligning them with heretics if they are not in fact heretical (1 Tim. 5:19). Remember, heresy does not refer to differences of opinion on debatable matters, but to denial of the core doctrines of Christianity, those doctrines which divide between Christian and non-Christian, saint and apostate.

When Christians who love God participate in unfair name-calling or heresy-branding, they unwittingly participate in the works of the pagans. Psalm 50:20–21 describes nonbelievers this way: "You sit and speak against your brother; you slander your own mother's son. These things you have done, and I kept silent; you thought that I was altogether like you; but I will reprove you, and set them in order before your eyes."

Within the context of Christian unity and brotherhood (based on the essential doctrines of biblical faith), the apostle Paul urges:

> Let no corrupt communication proceed out of your mouth, but what is good for necessary edification, that it may impart grace to the hearers. And do not grieve the Holy Spirit of God, by whom you were sealed for the day of redemption. Let all bitterness, wrath, anger, clamor, and evil speaking be put away from you, with all malice. And be kind to one another, tenderhearted, forgiving one another, just as God in Christ also forgave you (Eph. 4:29–32).

DO "NEW AGE" WORDS PROVE HERESY?

Witch hunting principles are unacceptable for Christians committed to biblical integrity.

One of the ways witch hunting purports to "discern heretics" is by testing the vocabularies people use. According to witch hunting methodology, one should be able to discern between heretic and believer by his or her choice of words.

Constance Cumbey, in *Hidden Dangers of the Rainbow,* says, "[Tom Sine] uses the phrase 'New Age' itself approximately 150 times in his book, more than even Marilyn Ferguson in *The Aquarian Conspiracy.*"[7]

Passport magazine, from Calvary Chapel of West Covina (California), indicted the Vineyard Christian churches in "John Wimber and the Vineyard Ministries."[8] One of the clues readers were given to help them discern the errors of the Vineyard was stated this way:

> John Wimber's teachings about "paradigm shifts" and "worldviews" sound familiar in many ways to the evangelistic efforts of the New Age movement to lead converts into Eastern mysticism. New Agers also attack Western Christianity as being a product of Western "rationalism" and "scientism."[9]

Should we consider Calvary Chapel of West Covina a part of the New Age Movement because this article itself uses "paradigm shifts" and "worldviews"? Of course not! Just as we should check the context of *Passport*'s use of the words, so the article should have presented the context within which the Vineyard used those terms before making a condemnation or even an innuendo.

THE IMPORTANCE OF CONTEXT

In an interview critical of Hunt's *Seduction,* we noted the importance of rejecting strict materialism and of experiencing spiritual reality with the biblical God:

Because we live in a "developed" Western country, we're materialistically oriented. We do away with things that are metaphysical or mystical. I personally like having things scientifically verifiable, but God came to me in a powerful, real, and metaphysical way, and saved me. Every one of us has to have that metaphysical experience with Jesus or we're not saved.[10]

Hunt responded to our statement by saying,

. . . as a cult expert, [Bob Passantino] ought to know how confusing it is to speak of the necessity of a "metaphysical experience with Jesus" in view of the meaning given this word (in spite of any dictionary definitions) by occultists and the Mind Science cults, who all consider their churches to be "metaphysical."[11]

How could Hunt so obviously ignore the context within which we used *metaphysical,* and the meaning ascribed by the context itself? With witch hunting practices, the argument would go that since we used *metaphysical* and occultists and Mind Science cults use *metaphysical,* we are unwittingly misleading our readers, making them vulnerable to the seduction of New Ageism. This in spite of the fact that we used the term in a thoroughly biblical way and in clear distinction to the way New Agers use the term.

Philosophy also uses the term *metaphysical* to refer to ultimate reality. Why should we let occultists and New Agers monopolize the use of perfectly good words that Christians have used for years? There was a time when "Christian" meant a believer in

Christ according to the Scriptures. Because of careless use by others, now we have to qualify what we mean by saying, "born-again Christian," or "evangelical Christian," or "Bible-believing, conservative, fundamentalist, evangelical, born-again, spirit-filled, etc., Christian." Why do we let the world take over and dilute or redefine perfectly good words and elbow us out of the way?

good!

THE ABSURDITIES OF WITCH HUNTING

Some ridiculous examples of misidentifying heretics by vocabulary occur in *When Your Money Fails*[12] and *The New Money System*,[13] both by Mary Stewart Relfe. Did you know that the Armstrong flooring company is a part of the antichrist religion? On page 28 of *When Your Money Fails* Relfe reproduced a picture of an Armstrong flooring tile stamped with style number 66613. The caption read, "Copy of section of floor tile, made in the U.S., prefixed on both sides with the number '666.' This depicts the '666' system in the United States Economy." With this kind of thinking, we might soon be asked to remove Psalm 66:6 from the Bible!

VOCABULARY BANNED FROM CHRISTIAN USE

We can laugh about some of the more extreme witch hunting practices, but it hits close to home when almost any Christian could be labeled a heretic merely by his or her vocabulary. The following is a list of "New Age" words we have collected from a number of New Age critics who identify heresy by vocabulary. Many of these critics even refer to them as "buzz words," and warn their audiences that they can identify New Agers by their use of these buzz words.

age of Aquarius	linear thinking	organism
celebration	matrix	paradigm
conspiracy	mechanistic	planetary initiations
crowded planet	metaphysical	rainbow
dualistic	mind science	rebirthing
global network	movement	reincarnation
global thread	mystical	right/left/whole brain
global village	neo-gnosticism	spaceship earth
hierarchy	networking	The Plan
human potential movement	networks	transformation
hypnosis	new age movement	transmission
initiation	new root race	visions
interdependent	new vision	(w)holistic
karma	new world order	worldview

Some of these words are used primarily in non-Christian or anti-Christian ways and may sometimes give a general indication that their users are promoting perspectives contrary to Christianity. (We cannot say their users and phrases are promoting non-Christian *worldviews* or we, too, could be condemned by somebody as heretics.) Such terms include age of Aquarius, new root race, neo-gnosticism, mind science, human potential movement, karma, and reincarnation.

However, when we see these terms we need to be careful. In a book against the New Age Movement, a Christian author wrote facetiously, "Despite all that I have said so far, I must confess that I do believe in reincarnation."[14] Although we might successfully argue that such a statement is confusing—perhaps even misleading—the author was not actually talking about reincarnation, as the context of his statement clearly shows. He was stating his biblical belief in the final resurrection, Christ being the firstfruits. One day, like Christ, we will be raised from the dead with glorified, immortal, perfect bodies. This is far different than the concept of reincarnation.

Words have both equivocal and univocal meanings. Equivocal means to have more than one meaning. Univocal means having one meaning only. Words are generally equivocal in isolation, univocal in context. For example, *table* is equivocal by itself. But it becomes univocal in context: "Hand me the mathematical table"; "The water table is low from the drought"; "Fix the wobbly leg on the table so I can serve dinner."

New Age buzz words are like any other words—generally neutral until they are used in a particular context. *Paradigm* means "framework" and can be used in a New Age way ("We must understand the world within the paradigm that we are all God"), a neutral way ("Explain the paradigm you used to understand your scientific observation"), or even a Christian way ("By accepting the paradigm that salvation is only through Jesus Christ, we can reject any other religion that offers a different plan of salvation").

DO YOU SOUND LIKE A NEW AGER?

Watch out if you work in the television industry. You might have to write a memo referring to a major television network—*network* is a New Age buzz word.

Watch out if you believe your physical health is tied to your spiritual and emotional health. You might use the world *holistic* to describe your attitude—but that is New Age too.

Watch out if you have to leave a note for your spouse saying you are taking your car into the shop for transmission service—the New Agers use *transmission* to refer to their own esoteric system of communication and conversion.

Watch out that you never share leads or connections with other Christians. You might be accused of "networking"—something prevalent in the New Age Movement.

Watch out for how your involvement against abortion is reported. You might be classified as a member of the pro-life *movement*—a favorite New Age buzz word.

Watch out if you serve in the armed forces, especially if you are in a leadership capacity. You might find it necessary to explain *the plan* for military *strategy*—an echo of Alice Bailey's New Age world conversion strategy known as The Plan.

Watch out when you try to describe how world economics, politics, and communication have affected our ability to evangelize the world for Christ. You might be tempted to use descriptions like "global village" or "crowded planet"—and people will brand you as a New Ager.

Watch out if you are a pastor performing a wedding ceremony. If you refer to Christ's miracle at the wedding feast at Cana, you might slip and call it a "celebration"—people might think you're a New Ager using a favorite New Age code word referring to the joy of being divine.

Watch out when you are counseling a new Christian on how the Holy Spirit's work in sanctification will cause his spirit to be changed, a *transformation*—a New Age goal.

Watch out when you water your lawn on a bright sunny day. Not only do you risk sunburned grass, you might inadvertently create a "rainbow"—your neighbors will think you're trying to secretly signal New Agers.

These are ridiculous examples, but they illustrate the fallacy fairly. Using New Age buzz words as a measuring stick for New Ageism is wholly inadequate. Words have meaning in context and it is simplistic to the point of blind ignorance to witch hunt by vocabulary.

NEW AGE WORD STATISTICS

We earlier mentioned Cumbey's declaration that author Tom Sine had connections to the New Age Movement because he used the term *New Age* more than 150 times in one of his books. Well, we counted the number of times Cumbey used *New Age* in *The Hidden Dangers of the Rainbow* and found that she used it 178 times in just the first six chapters! Obviously, she was *criticizing* the New Age Movement, and the frequency with which she used the term is irrelevant. But so also is the frequency with which Sine used the term. We do not agree with much of Sine's economic, political, and theological interpretations and ideas, but it is not fair to condemn him by word statistics. Significant would be *ideas in context* from Sine that would inexorably tie him into the New Age.

NEW AGE AGENDAS

On page 154 of *Hidden Dangers* Cumbey produced evidence she said showed the connections between Christian relief and development organization World Vision and its president, Stanley Mooneyham, with the New Age Movement. She quoted Mooneyham to show what he had in common with the New Age Movement. In the quote, Mooneyham urged the formation of community "family planning services," and urged open forum discussions on "birth control, abortion, artificial insemination, genetic control, and death control."

To Cumbey, this indicates Mooneyham's *endorsement* of all of these practices. But nowhere did she prove it. In fact, she could be indicted by this same line of reasoning. As a trial lawyer, Cumbey was a member and officer of the National Association of Women Lawyers which at that same time actively endorsed, supported, and published literature in favor of women's rights to abortion. Without asking Cumbey's own position on abortion, however, it would be unfair of anyone to accuse her of supporting abortion as she has accused Mooneyham. On our Answers In Action radio program, we have presented open forum discussions on abortion, euthanasia, AIDS, and other issues. However, we are and always have been totally against abortion, euthanasia, sexual promiscuity, and homosexual practices. There is a vast difference between urging discussion and giving an endorsement.

WITCH HUNTING UNFAIRLY BRANDS NEW AGERS, CHRISTIANS, AND EVEN THE BIBLE

Through these chapters we have seen many examples of witch hunting. New Agers and other nonbelievers certainly are not justified simply because we criticize witch hunting. It is not a matter of letting the guilty defendant go free because of a technicality. It is not an either/or situation. God says "test all things" (2 Thess. 5:21), but he does not approve bad tests. God has given us reasonable scriptural tests wholly adequate for convicting the guilty and protecting the innocent.

Witch hunting brands all alike: New Agers or other nonbelievers for the wrong reasons and Christians for the wrong reasons. Even the Bible could be targeted by witch hunting.

THE BIBLE AS A NEW AGE HANDBOOK

After the many examples we have shown, it is not too incredible to believe that witch hunting standards, if turned loose, could even attack the Bible itself. Here is how even the Bible could be misconstrued as a New Age Handbook, if witch hunting methods are used to analyze it.

Uses new age symbols (rainbow)	*Genesis 9:13*
	Revelation 10:1
Promotes a new world order	*Revelation 21:1–4*
Uses the term "transformation"	*Romans 12:1–2*
Reports mystical experiences	*Matthew 17:1–13*
Encourages re-birthing	*John 3:5*
Records out-of-body experiences	*2 Corinthians 12:3*

Reports visions and trances	*Revelation 1:9ff*
Claims secret knowledge	*Revelation 10:4*
	1 Corinthians 2:7
	Ephesians 3:9
Threatens destruction for all	
who will not submit	*Matthew 25:46*
Has a global network	*Matthew 28:19*
Promises members immortality	*John 8:51*
Looking for one world leader	*Titus 2:13*
Purports divine revelations	*2 Peter 1:19–21*
Advocates forehead mark for	
identifying members	*Revelation 7:3; 22:4*
Promotes eventual zero	
population growth	*Matthew 22:30*
Promotes use of incense	*Revelation 8:4*
Promotes world ecological control	*Genesis 1:26, 28*
Claims supernatural healing power	*James 5:14–15*

The context of each of these verses, combined with a reasonable analysis of the meaning, more than adequately vindicates the Bible from the charges of New Ageism. Most who fall into using witch hunting tactics to identify New Agers are sincerely attempting to reveal heresy and preserve orthodoxy. The last thing they would like to do is attack the Bible, which they sincerely hold as the standard against which everything should be judged. However, their heavy-handed weapon wielding ends up snaring Christians and even the Bible, as well as bonafide New Agers.

Perhaps one of the saddest results of bad discernment was related to us in a personal conversation with Tim Brown, former director of the Colossian Fellowship cult apologetics ministry in Seattle,

Washington. Brown sees a lot of Christians who have been hurt by heresy and unbiblical teachings within Christian churches. He knows from firsthand counseling the dangers of New Ageism in the Church.

He also knows how some of these same people fail to get the help they need because they have been turned off by witch hunting. He said,

> When somebody knows that the pastor or church he's reading about isn't really the way the book says, that book loses all of its credibility. I've seen people who really needed help in rejecting New Age ideas they got from other Christians and churches, but who wouldn't believe anything some of these books say, because they see things that are twisted or just not true in them. The very people the book was especially meant to help can't get the help because the book's flaws have ruined its credibility.

We do not know of any Christian who, if a friend is in trouble, does not want to help in the best way possible. Perhaps you have a friend who has swallowed heresy of one kind or another. Perhaps someone in your family is in a cult. Maybe members of your congregation are caught up in an unbiblical psychological pseudo-biblical fad. You do not have to be a professional cult apologist to care enough to get involved. And each of us, professional or not, has a Christian obligation to get involved in promoting the truth of the gospel above all else.

When we understand and can communicate the truth of the gospel, we do not need untrustworthy witch hunting techniques. Far from helping us, they can, as Tim Brown found out, actually drive away the very people who need help so desperately. We cannot let our carelessness compromise our critical integrity and drive away those who are hurting.

People They're Slandering

*T*here are many who, innocent or guilty, have been targeted by witch hunting tactics. The targets we have chosen to highlight in the next three chapters have been chosen primarily because their situations provide the best illustrations of the problems inherent in witch hunting. These targets are not necessarily innocent on all counts, but they have been unfairly "wounded" by witch hunting weapons. The many targets we did not choose to mention are not necessarily guilty—we simply couldn't cover them all.

The individuals chosen for our evaluation in this chapter are Christian psychologist Dr. James Dobson (founder of Focus on the Family) and Prosperity pastor Casey Treat (Christian Faith Center, Seattle, Washington). We will highlight some of the most significant accusations against these two individuals as representative of what witch hunting can do to individuals.

DR. JAMES DOBSON

The Charges

Dr. James Dobson has been accused of neglecting the gospel, teaching the heretical notion of self-esteem, denying the sinfulness of man, and promoting the inherently ungodly "religion" of psychology.[1]

The Background

The *Los Angeles Times* described Dr. James Dobson and his radio program, "Focus on the Family":

> Since he began broadcasting in 1977, Dr. James C. Dobson's "Focus on the Family" has become the second most popular radio program (in a number of stations) behind Paul Harvey's "News and Commentary." From 43 stations 9 years ago, "Focus on the Family" has spread to 970 stations in 17 countries today, and it's still growing. . . .
>
> The reason for such growth?
>
> "The family is under severe stress today," says Dobson simply. "Our reason for existence is to help preserve the institution of the family."[2]

Dobson's ministry is a Christian ministry, based on essential Christian doctrine and emphasizing Christian family values such as the sanctity of human life, the integrity of nuclear families, marital fidelity, and Christian discipleship. In addition to its multi-faceted media ministry, "Focus on the Family" also provides materials and financial aid to other groups dealing with similar problems.

Dr. Dobson is the author of numerous books, articles, pamphlets, teaching cassettes, and teaching videos. He has been heralded by dozens of Christian churches, organizations, and periodicals as America's leading champion of Christian family values.

James Dobson and "Focus on the Family" are not perfect. They cannot and do not claim to represent all of normative Christianity to the world. There are some ideas and emphases held by Dobson with which other Christians might not agree. However, by essential doctrine and by fruit, Dobson has proved that he and his organization are well within biblical orthodoxy.

The Evaluation

Most of the witch hunting accusations against James Dobson concern two main themes: (1) he is a "Christian psychologist," which is a contradiction in terms; and (2) he advocates "self-esteem," which contradicts the biblical teaching of the depravity (utter sinfulness) of mankind.

Some Christians sincerely believe that *all* psychology is anti-Christian, unbiblical. We saw in Chapter 6 how Dave Hunt views "Christian psychology":

"Christian psychology" represents the most deadly and at the same time the most appealing and popular form of *modernism* ever to confront the church. . . .[3]

Christian psychology could almost be described as a cult inside the church. It has its own vocabulary, an endless new category of problems tagged with labels not found in the Bible and unknown to the church in its entire history. . . . In short, this cult has its own gospel, its own religious rituals administered by its own class of priests, the Christian psychologists, who have gained authority over those who only know God's Word. . . .[4]

While Hunt (almost paradoxically) does not dismiss all of Dobson's ministry,[5] others who engage in witch hunting are not so charitable. The logical implications of Hunt's attitude toward Christian psychology is revealed by a letter writer to a radio station which carried Dobson's daily program:

> Then we come to Dobson's theology of self-esteem. You may try to distinguish it from secular self-esteem, but it is fundamentally flawed. First of all, why is Dobson using the same word that the secularists are using? This obviously causes confusion to Christians. Second, Dobson is a psychologist who has developed his theology of self-esteem from his experience as a child psychologist and his personal life.[6]

Keep in mind that this book is not a treatise on psychology. We will not sidetrack our main thesis to dig into the controversy about psychology and biblical truth. In line with the purpose of this book, we are concerned with examining whether or not Dobson has been the victim of witch hunting, not whether he has *successfully* integrated the Bible and psychology.

Dr. Dobson's statements, from his early books through to today, consistently reveal his commitment to the Bible and Christianity as the *foundation* for every human endeavor—psychology, counseling, and the Focus on the Family ministry itself. The letter writer quoted above tried to force Dobson's ideas and ministry away from any biblical foundation and guessed that Dobson owed the secular world for everything.

Contrast that unproved assumption with Dobson's clear statement in one of his early books, *The Strong-Willed Child:*

The underlying principles expressed herein are not my own innovative insights which would be forgotten in a brief season or two. Instead, they originated with the inspired biblical writers who gave us the foundation for all relationships in the home. . . .

My purpose has been nothing more ambitious than to verbalize the Judeo-Christian tradition regarding discipline of children and to apply those concepts to today's families. . . . I did not invent it, nor can I change it. My task has been merely to report what I believe to be the prescription of the Creator Himself.[7]

It is simply unfair to accuse Dobson, as a Christian psychologist, of promoting a rival religion when he plainly states that he has based his teaching, not on "his experience as a child psychologist and his personal life" but on *God's Word.*

It could be fair to challenge Dobson's interpretation of Scripture, which he believes provides for the legitimate integration of biblical truth with psychological principles. But that is a completely different matter from the charge that he depends on psychology instead of the Bible.

Other accusations against Dobson are that his teachings about self-esteem come from a secular worldview, deny the biblical doctrine of the depravity (sinfulness) of mankind, and insulate people from their need to turn to Jesus Christ for salvation.

Martin and Deidre Bobgan quote Dobson several times concerning self-esteem in their book *Psycho-Heresy* and conclude,

Low self-esteem is popular because it's much easier to accept the idea of having "low self-esteem" than confessing evil, ungodly, self-centered thoughts and then repenting through believing what God has said in

His Word. Low self-esteem calls for psychological treatment to raise the self-esteem. . . . We would suggest that one look to Scripture to discover one's greatest need and to find an antidote to life's problems, rather than to attempt to scripturalize some psychological fad.[8]

The same sentiments are echoed in Hunt's *Seduction*[9] and *Beyond Seduction.*[10]

Some critics of "Christian" self-esteem take Dobson's statements about human *worth* as meaning that somehow fallen man has *merit* or something in him that causes him to deserve salvation. However, Dobson, along with many other Christian psychologists, reserves the use of worth to mean the reflective value all humans have *as beings created in God's image and as recipients of his love.* This does not imply any inherent goodness or sinlessness, which could be described as merit. Christian psychologist Dr. John Carter makes this clear:

Man has fallen into sin and thus God's image in man has become marred, warped, or distorted. It is never lost, and it is being renewed through personal appropriation of salvation in Christ (Eph. 4:24; Col. 3:10).[11]

Even though secular psychologists would never accept this view of man's sinfulness and redemption, and even though some who call themselves Christian psychologists really *do* mean that man has inherent merit and is not utterly fallen, even many strict anti-psychology Christian critics would agree with Carter's statement.

This is the same position Dobson takes. Dobson should not be accused of promoting unbiblical self-esteem simply because he uses the term or emphasizes the very real, but marred, image of God in fallen man. Dobson *also* teaches the sinfulness of man, the complete inability to find human fulfillment or salvation outside of a personal, regenerating encounter with the Lord Jesus Christ and acceptance of his sacrifice for our sins on the cross. Here is how Dobson put it in one of his earliest books, and this same sentiment is echoed in his later writings:

> I'm sure you will find great warmth, love, and acceptance from God when you pray that prayer. By doing so, you are saying, "I want Your will for my life, not because I'm a superstar or superman or superwoman, but because You promised to help those who admit their weaknesses. I'm depending on *Your* power and *Your* strength to make something beautiful out of my life." The Bible teaches us to reveal this humble dependence on the Lord, and He will honor it!
>
> . . . In fact, God loves you and me so much that He actually sent His only Son to die for us. Now that's real love at its greatest![12]

Lest there be any lingering doubt concerning Dobson's stance regarding man's need for salvation, here is what he said on a broadcast of "Focus on the Family":

> All of us have to answer that awesome question: What will we do with this Jesus who is called the Christ?
>
> . . . The responsibility for accepting that salvation rests squarely on our shoulders. Hebrews 2:3 says "How shall we escape if we neglect so great a salvation?" If we turn our backs on this merciful remedy, there's not a chance of our escaping the damnation that we deserve, because *there is no other remedy; there's no other plea; there's no other cure—apart from Jesus Christ. There is no other way, but to depend on the salvation he has provided.*[13]

Dobson went on to explain that this salvation is received by calling on the name of the Lord and repenting from our sins. Then he led any listener who wished to receive Christ in a prayer:

> Lord, I bring to you my sinful nature today as you've revealed it to me. And I know that I have nothing to offer you that could earn your forgiveness and love, but you've offered your son Jesus as a free gift to me. And I want him as the Lord of my life. I want to serve him and obey him and follow him. You have my life, you have my family. You have my past and my present and my future. And you are my possessor and my dispossessor. And from this moment forward I am your child. Thank you for loving me and forgiving me and making me your own. Amen.[14]

We have many disagreements with secular psychology and psychologists; in many ways secular psychology is a rival to a Christian worldview. And many who claim to be using Christian psychology have done little more than dress up secular psychology in Christian terminology. However, there are some Christian psychologists who claim they can maintain a strict fidelity to God's Word and the cardinal doctrines of Christianity while separating the wheat from the chaff in psychology. Consistently throughout his ministry, James Dobson declares that his ministry is based on his understanding of the Bible's foundational truths. Some may disagree with his understanding, but it is witch hunting to accuse him of basing his ministry on secular psychology and of denying one's need of salvation in Jesus Christ.

PASTOR CASEY TREAT

Pastor Casey Treat has been accused of fostering the heresy of Satan's lie in Genesis 3:5, teaching his followers that they are gods and "exact duplicates of God."

The Background

This is one section of the book that we are somewhat reluctant to write. Pastor Casey Treat and his Christian Faith Center (Seattle, Washington) actively promote some teachings and practices with which we strongly disagree. The Christian Faith Center is heavily involved in the Prosperity Movement (material prosperity is your divine right and a sign of God's blessing); healing in the atonement teachings (physical healing is your divine right); positive confession (you can manipulate and/or create in the physical world with your words spoken "in faith"); unscriptural visualization (you can manipulate reality through mental imagery); and the advocacy and sale of books and authors who promote these ideas. We cannot agree with any of this.

However, Treat and Christian Faith Center have been accused unfairly or untruthfully in some instances, and this is contrary to the biblical pattern of discernment.

The Bible consistently teaches that the Lord's people should judge honestly; our attitude toward truth will reflect our relationship with the Lord. Second Corinthians 13:8 asserts, "For we can do nothing against the truth, but for the truth." Philippians 1:9–10 explains that proper judgment gives us the security of knowing we are exercising the fruit of righteousness through Jesus Christ: "And this I pray, that your love may abound still more and more in knowledge and all discernment, that you may approve the things that are excellent, that you may be sincere and without offense until the day of Christ."

It is tempting to let false accusations stand when we are convinced that Casey Treat and Christian Faith Center are promoting unbiblical practices and beliefs. *But it is not right.* For example, the accusations brought against Treat by Dave Hunt in *The Seduction of Christianity* are unfair. It is never right to do wrong to accomplish a "good" end. (In the study of ethics this is called "utilitarianism" or "situational ethics." Whatever works and achieves the desired end, is justified and "good." Christian ethics should never be utilitarian or situational.)

Tim Brown, former director of The Colossian Fellowship, noted,

> The Colossian Fellowship is not against David Hunt or his new book, for it is a timely and in-depth study into new problems within the Christian church. Nor are we defending Rev. Treat, for we strongly disagree with several of his teachings. We are trying to take a neutral stand for the truth on this one situation as we perceive it at this time.

> David's book *The Seduction of Christianity* on the whole appears to be a great work; but now, we can only wonder—why does he deliberately continue in this misunderstanding?[15]

The Charges

In *Seduction,*[16] Hunt (properly) includes Treat with other positive confession teachers such as Norman Grubb, Bill Volkman, Paul Yonggi Cho, Charles Capps, and Fred Price. In fact, when Colossian Fellowship asked Treat to name "the most influential pastor in your life," Treat responded, "I guess it would be Fred Price of Crenshaw Christian Center in California. His teachings (mainly for his prosperity doctrine) and ministry have really been a blessing to me."[17]

However, Hunt also charges Treat with Mormonism's error of repeating Satan's lie in the Garden of Eden, that is, that men are or can be gods. He bases this on Treat's suggestion to his congregation "that they were gods"[18] and his "teaching that we are gods." Hunt buttresses his charges by quoting from a tape of one of Treat's sermons. The portion Hunt quotes certainly sounds heretical. Treat says, for example, "I'm an exact duplicate of God, When God looks in the mirror, He sees me! When I look in the mirror, I see God!" and "Since I'm an exact duplicate of God, I'm going to act like God!"[19]

Heresy or Ignorance?

But there is a problem cult watchers often encounter: when is a teacher actively promoting error and when is he theologically ignorant, ill-advised, untrained, or sloppy? In other words, heresy and ignorance are two different causes although both can produce bad beliefs. Our response to deliberate heretics should be swift with the stern judgment of God's Word. Our response to ignorance and irresponsibility, however, should be with gentle exhortation, lovingly explaining the truth to a brother in sin.

We should follow the New Testament pattern exemplified by Priscilla and Aquila in Acts 18:26, when they gently corrected the ignorance of Apollos, who "knew only the baptism of John" (Acts 18:25): "When Aquila and Priscilla heard him, they took him aside and explained to him the way of God more accurately."

When someone claims to be a Christian pastor and claims to have orthodox doctrine, then Christian apologists have the obligation to investigate carefully both the charges and the defense. Only when overwhelming evidence in favor of the charges warrant it (1 Tim. 5:19) and the one claiming to be a brother is given sufficient admonishment and opportunity to change but refuses (Matt. 18:15–16), should we feel free to accuse him openly (Matt. 18:17).

The Colossian Fellowship's Role

The Colossian Fellowship, directed by Timothy Brown, was an apologetics ministry in the Northwest (Seattle, Washington) which disbanded at the end of 1987. Through research, writing, lectures, seminars, and interviews, Colossian Fellowship provided active biblical judgment especially focused on cult activities in the Northwest. The Colossian Fellowship has done the most extensive research and publication on a Seattle area cult, Community Chapel, and its leader, Donald Barnett.

In late 1984, Colossian Fellowship began inquiries concerning Casey Treat and his Seattle area Christian Faith Center. Their June 1985 journal report provided the first in-depth, carefully researched, and biblically based report on Treat and his church.

Included were a carefully chronicled history of the church and background of Treat; a well-documented investigative article on the intricate web behind Christian Faith Center, Washington Drug Rehabilitation Center, and Julius Young Ministries; a good summary of the biblical view of prosperity and positive confession; an even-handed interview with Treat; a review of Treat's book *Renewing the Mind;* and background information on the Prosperity

Movement. This report, instigated by the queries Colossian Fellowship had received, concluded that some rumors were false, some were true, and that there were other areas of concern uncovered for the first time in their investigation. Treat and Christian Faith Center (CFC) did not emerge unscathed.

However, Colossian Fellowship director Brown was concerned that the criticisms of Treat and CFC that Hunt was planning to use in *Seduction* were false. If Hunt were going to accuse Treat, reasoned Brown, he at least should investigate his claim to be an orthodox Christian, confront him with the accusations, hear his defense, and then publicly accuse him only of those heretical things he could prove Treat was promoting knowingly.

Brown wrote Hunt a five-page letter on May 15, 1985, before *Seduction* was published, detailing where he thought Hunt was unfairly accusing Treat and urging Hunt to investigate more thoroughly:

> We would, again, like to encourage you to contact him, so as to ensure that anything you say and write is true, accurate, and current. As you are well aware, when one discernment writer fails to write what is true, accurate, and current, and his errors are discovered—all discernment writers and ministries suffer.[20]

Hunt's response, according to Brown,[21] was adamant: he felt no need or obligation to contact Treat or to modify his accusations. He gave five reasons: (1) he couldn't afford to contact everyone; (2) he assumed that the people he criticized were too busy to make time for him; (3) those he criticized probably wouldn't let him past their secretaries; (4) what they said publicly was open to public criticism and review, no matter who they were (or claimed to be), even

Christians; and (5) even if they had changed their beliefs, Hunt still had to rescue those who had been seduced by their former words.

Hunt Meets Treat

Hunt was already scheduled to speak in the Seattle area June 12–14, 1985, so Colossian Fellowship arranged a meeting between Hunt and Treat. During their meeting on June 12, Hunt brought up his major charges to Treat and Treat responded. The following is the result of that encounter: Hunt decided that his initial accusations were justified; Treat admitted sloppiness but denied heresy; and Colossian Fellowship concluded, based on their own investigation of Treat's previous statements and his statements to Hunt, that Treat had been unjustly accused by Hunt *on this subject of "little gods."* Because of his concerns, Brown circulated copies of a subsequent letter from Hunt:

> I don't think that any reasonable person, after reading that [quote on pages 82 and 83 of *Seduction* quoting Treat] could possibly accept Casey's explanation that you [Tim Brown] not only naively accept but insist I must accept also. . . . There is no "context" (certainly none in that sermon) that can explain away such statements. . . . If Casey doesn't mean we are gods when he so clearly says it repeatedly, then how can you or I be sure that he means we aren't gods when he says that?

> . . . I am not dealing with Casey as an isolated case, but as part of the Positive Confession Movement. . . . My quote of Casey in *Seduction* is lengthy and exact, certainly NOT a misrepresentation of what he said. In spite of his denial, does he not continue to invite to speak at his church and exclusively carry the books of

men who teach that we are gods? Has Casey made any attempt to communicate to purchasers of that tape and to his congregation that he didn't mean what he so clearly said? Has he discontinued carrying books that teach this, and warned his congregation against this teaching?

I can't take his denials seriously until he does this, even though I told him I believe he was sincere during our discussion.[22]

The Evaluation

Treat defended himself against the "little gods" charge both to the Colossian Fellowship and also directly to Dave Hunt. In summary, his defense was that (1) he didn't mean anything heretical by his reference to Christians as gods; (2) someone he trusted told him the Hebrew of Genesis 1:26's "in our image" meant "an exact duplicate"; and (3) he did not use the term "gods" in either the way Mormons use the term or the way Satan supposedly meant it in Genesis 3:5.

Here is what he said, in part, to the Colossian Fellowship in an interview before his meeting with Dave Hunt.

I used that [phrase "exact duplicate of God"] in a teaching some time ago [fall of 1983], and whenever I teach in that area now, I explain it more carefully. I was told by a pastor [Charles Capps], and I felt that he had an understanding of Hebrew, that when the term "in his likeness," or "in his image" is used, that he is talking about an exact duplicate in kind. Not that we are God. . . .

And I see where if a person was looking for something, they could use that. I think that if they listen

151

> to the whole message, they would understand that I teach, and I believe, that without God, we are nothing. We are going to have to be born again, if we want eternal life, and come to Jesus. And we will never be divine, we will never be God, or the Father.

> We are never going to evolve into God. . . . I'm trying to teach that we are part of God's family. God has created us to be his children. . . .[23]

The *Prevue* article summarized Treat's teaching that "he believed we were 'gods' in a generational sense, that is, that just as dogs have puppies and cats have kittens, 'If God has a child, it is a God. As a teaching, it is to show that we are not worms; we are God's children, we are made in his image, and God's class.'"[24]

Clear biblical teaching is completely contrary to this. The Bible never refers to humans as "gods" except as a pagan's false opinion; or in reference to human agency representing God or fulfilling God's will—Aaron to Pharaoh; the (evil) judges to the people in Psalm 82. In addition, the Bible makes it very clear that there is a distinction between God's nature and man's nature (Rom. 1:23). We are *adopted* children of God (Rom. 8:15) through the salvific agency of Jesus, who is the unique Son of God, the only begotten Son of God (John 1:14,18).

However, Treat is distinguishing his own belief from both that of the Mormons and that of Satan's supposed lie in Genesis 3:5. We do not agree with Treat's position, but we do not believe he is teaching that man can grow into godhood through works (Mormonism) or that man is somehow equal to God ("Satan's lie").[25]

Here is how Treat defended himself when he met Hunt face-to-face:

If you interpreted me literally, I would have to laugh. . . . we are children of God and that makes us different than monkeys, different than dogs, different than worms—not unworthy things, but children of God. That was the point of the whole lesson. I think that if you listened, you would have to agree that that is the point. . . . as Paul says in Philippians, "I can do all things through Christ and yet without Christ, I'm nothing. . . ."

[Treat was then asked if he was "aspiring that we're gods, in any way, shape, or form."] No. Nothing like that at all.[26]

Colossian Fellowship does not usually come to the defense of those with whom it strongly disagrees. In fact, Colossian Fellowship was very critical of Treat and Christian Faith Center in both its June and September 1985 *Prevue* journals. They biblically criticized his positive confession, prosperity, and aberrant three-part salvation teachings. But they were strongly convinced that Hunt had made an inadequate case for indicting Treat as an incipient Mormon or Hindu in his theology. In defending Treat, Colossian Fellowship was willing to take the risk of being misconstrued as approving of Treat, his teachings, and his ministry. They summarized their objections in a letter to *Seduction*'s publisher, Harvest House:

David [Hunt] recently questioned Casey Treat, "What would you expect a reasonable person to think when you say that?" We ask you, in the context of this section of David's book, what would you expect a reasonable reader to think when he quotes Casey and writes of Satan's lie and Mormonism? From this section of the book, they could only understand that Casey Treat and his members believe in some form of Mor-

> monism and that they really believe that they are gods.
>
> We have interviewed many current and former members of Casey Treat's church and we have not found one who believes any sort of the thing that David implies—NOT ONE. Casey's recent book, *Renewing the Mind,* doesn't teach this sort of thing either. Casey Treat denied it to us and denied it to David Hunt. . . .
>
> If David feels this section on Casey Treat must remain in the book, why not clarify, by quoting Casey himself, what Casey meant by this sermon? Then if the reader wishes to ignore what Casey has said in explanation, then David is not guilty of misrepresentation.[27]

What is our perspective on the tangled Casey Treat situation? Like Colossian Fellowship, we do not like defending someone who promotes error, especially when they do it in the name of Christ. However, also like Colossian Fellowship, we do not believe Hunt has properly defined or proved Treat's "little god" teaching, or shown adequate concern for doing so.

SHARP SHOTS OR CHEAP SHOTS?

Witch hunting uses critical weapons sometimes against real enemies, sometimes against the ignorantly wrong, and, unfortunately, sometimes even against the innocent. We believe that Hunt has wrongly used a weapon against someone who, at best, is ignorantly wrong. Even if Treat is a "real enemy," it is not fair to "convict him on a technicality."

We do not always disagree with Dave Hunt. We

agree that many of the people and teachings he has criticized in *Seduction, Beyond Seduction,* and even in *Whatever Happened to Heaven?*[28] should be criticized. And we would have been closer to agreement with Hunt if he had criticized Treat for selling and actively promoting the books and materials of other authors who more clearly affirm the heretical "little gods" doctrine, which criticism Hunt made in his September 1985 letter to Brown.

It would be nice if everything were black and white. It would be easy if heretics were always deliberate, if all "little god" heresies—Mormon, Hindu, Gnostic, New Age, Prosperity—were equivalent, if a cheap shot were just as valuable as an accurate shot.

But reality is not like that. Witch hunting typically sees everything as either/or, black or white, all good or all bad. The reality about Casey Treat is that (1) he is wrong and unbiblical about what he teaches but perhaps partly because of his own inadequate training and theology; (2) his "little gods" doctrine is not identical to Mormon or Hindu deification teachings; (3) thus Hunt's criticism of Treat in *Seduction* is inadequate; and (4) he could perhaps be more easily convicted of promoting error by his univocal endorsement of other Prosperity proponents. Careful judgment is especially necessary in a situation like this, where both unwarranted accusations and unmerited approval can affect thousands of the teacher's followers.

Tim Brown explained his concerns in a conversation with us:

> Treat's followers are especially vulnerable to the false teachings coming from Treat and from the many other leaders and teachers he actively promotes. They need the strong warnings of the Dave Hunts calling

for a return to biblical doctrine. But when he wrongly accuses their leader, he loses his credibility and they can't benefit from his accurate judgments. It's not worth losing their trust because maybe you were sloppy and didn't think it would matter, since you knew their leader was wrong anyway.[29]

Ironically, the very ones who need help the most resist help because they have been hurt by witch hunting methods. Witch hunting hurts its targets, whether they are legitimate targets or innocent victims. And it ends up hurting the very people it is designed to help.

In the next chapter we will see how witch hunting has sabotaged some organizations, and, as a consequence, affected whether or not some very needy people are helped.

CHAPTER 8

Groups They're Damaging

*R*ecently we were having lunch at a restaurant with some friends. Susan mentioned that she and her husband wanted to contribute to a relief organization that worked with disadvantaged children worldwide. "But we don't know what organization we should support," Susan complained, "you hear so much about all these relief agencies pocketing most of the money and the people not really getting helped. How can we know that our donation is really going to be used to help poor children?" We gave a few principles[1] and then the discussion turned more general, with everyone at the table mentioning different kinds of nonprofit organizations about which they had questions and doubts as to their integrity. The general consensus at the table was that "let the buyer beware" was still the best advice.

There are literally thousands of nonprofit religious organizations operating in the United States today. Despite the enormous publicity surrounding the televangelist scandals and the periodic revelations concerning some nonprofit organizations' misappropriation of funds, the vast majority of these organizations are serving sincerely and effectively both the Body of Christ and the world around them.

There are organizations dedicated to defending the unborn, championing minority rights, feeding the hungry, helping the poor, defending the faith, educating the illiterate. Some organizations are within the mainstream of organized American Christianity but may not have a clear-cut, evangelical, biblical commitment. Others guard their evangelical orthodoxy as an integral part of their ministry.

Sadly, a few organizations exist which are not what they claim to be. Sometimes the organization will say all the right things and look like an effective Christian ministry, but in actuality will be little more than a fund-raising center to feed the expensive tastes of its leaders. It is also sad that a few organizations, in an effort to get Christians' support, deceptively claim to be evangelical, while behind the scenes they really promote a New Age agenda and belief system.

Christians need to consider cautiously before they contribute time, money, or effort to any charitable organization (or even church). Conversely, Christians should also scrutinize carefully any charges *against* an organization before they dismiss the organization out of hand. Organizations are no less vulnerable to witch hunting techniques than are individuals.

THE JESUIT CONSPIRACY

Several years ago, when we were directing CARIS, we received a letter from someone named Roscoe in the Northeast. He said he had ordered materials from us for witnessing to the cults but had not received them. We wrote back that we had no record of his order or payment, but that if he would reorder and send a copy of his canceled check, we would be happy to replace his order and reimburse him for the extra postage and the copying cost for his check.

We did not hear from Roscoe, but we heard from our local Postal Inspector. Roscoe had lodged a formal complaint against us for mail fraud. Two reasons were listed on the complaint form. First, he repeated his claim that he had ordered materials and not received them. Second, he accused us of misrepresentation since we called ourselves a "counter-cult ministry" and yet we had no publications against what he termed "the biggest cult of all, the Great Whore of Babylon, the Roman Catholic Church."

It was easy to provide the Postal Inspector with copies of our correspondence asking for verification that his check had been cleared, and we went ahead and sent his order out without proof of payment (which we never did receive) just to go the extra mile.

Fortunately, the Postal Inspector did not require us to respond to him concerning Roscoe's second charge. He said that if he got involved in that, he would be violating separation of church and state and free speech. But we wanted to respond to Roscoe anyway.

Bob got his phone number from directory assistance and called him one evening. Their conversation quickly degenerated into Roscoe shouting epithets at Bob about CARIS's conspiracy with Roman Catholicism, and Bob trying in vain to reason with him. Then Roscoe's real objection came out. He was convinced that CARIS was actually a secret mission of the Roman Catholic Church, commissioned by the Jesuits to masquerade as a non-Catholic cult apologetics organization. In fact, Roscoe announced, he was convinced that Bob was a Jesuit in disguise!

Bob tried to reason with him. "Look, Roscoe, how can I be a Jesuit?"

"That's easy," Roscoe cut in, "Look at your last name—Passantino—that's Italian Catholic if I ever heard it!"

"But, Roscoe, you can talk to my mother. She'll tell you I haven't practiced Catholicism since I made my first communion. Talk to my pastor. He'll tell you I'm not a Catholic. And just because we don't have a tract against them and I don't think they're the Great Whore of Babylon doesn't prove I'm their secret agent, much less a Jesuit. Come on, Roscoe, Jesuits spend half their lives in Catholic schools and seminaries. They've taken vows of celibacy. Roscoe, I have a wife and children. I *can't* be a Jesuit!"

"Only a Jesuit would have such a clever disguise!" Roscoe hung up.

THE TARGETS

If witch hunting were always as easy to spot as Roscoe's, we wouldn't have written this book. Instead, most witch hunting, especially against organizations, is much more subtle and, in turn, much more damaging to its targets. In this chapter we will review witch hunting tactics used against four groups: Bread for the World, a national lobbying organization with special emphasis on the hunger issue; World Vision, a Christian international relief and development organization; the Coalition on Revival (COR), an interdenominational coalition of Christians concerned with recovering a Christian worldview as a basis for orthodox unity in Christ;

and the Reconstructionists, not actually an organization, but a loosely knit group of postmillennial Christians whose writings have caused controversy.

BREAD FOR THE WORLD

Bread for the World has been accused of being endorsed by the New Age Movement, not buying food for the hungry, and promoting an antichrist system of world food management.

The Background

Bread for the World describes itself as "a Christian citizens' movement in the USA." It does not claim to be fundamentalist or exclusively evangelical. It is not a relief organization as such, but works with American legislative bodies to promote famine relief on a worldwide basis. Its supporters, directors, and endorsers include non-Christians as well as Christians.

We do not necessarily endorse Bread for the World, and the charges listed below are serious, but we believe that the "proof" given to support the charges constitutes witch hunting rather than persuasive evidence.

The Charges

In numerous talks and in *Hidden Dangers of the Rainbow* Constance Cumbey cites Bread for the World for various failings, including being a New Age front organization; receiving endorsements from the New Age organization Lucis Trust; having as a board member a New Age leader, Gerhard Elston; and failing to use any of its money to buy food for starving people.

Bread for the World—[is] an organization that has managed to win at least two write-ups in Lucis Trust papers as "characteristic" of the New Group of World Servers. And, Bread for the World has never bought a grain of rice for anyone. Their monies are strictly spent for lobbying for national and international measures—including creation of global reserves and agencies to control the distribution of world assets.[2]

Wittingly or unwittingly, the program of Bread for the World and its teaching that one has a *duty* to support a New World Order (books distributed by you [Bread for the World] carry this theme), play right into the hands of the New Agers. And you have New Age leadership active on your board of directors . . . the direction in which it is headed is dangerous and . . . BFW has been co-opted by the Movement for its own purposes.[3]

We do not necessarily believe that government stockpiling is the best way to feed the starving. We are convinced that politics and economics have much more to do with famine in today's age of technological agriculture and worldwide shipping than does a lack of food production. And we would not endorse famine relief plans that would advance socialism and retard free enterprise.

However, we also believe that many sincere, Bible-believing, orthodox Christians have differing views on economics and famine relief and that they are honestly working to relieve worldwide human suffering in a workable, biblical way. We can say we do not agree. We can even say we do not think certain methods are biblical, but that does not give us license to accuse those with whom we disagree of New Age sympathies or ties.

The Evaluation

Cumbey has not been fair to extrapolate from Bread for the World's modest efforts at promoting multinational food reserves to a "one-world government machinery" or to "agencies to control the distribution of world assets." Bread for the World responded,

We wish you had taken time to contact us about your concerns regarding our organization. We feel some of our policies are misrepresented in your book and wish to clarify the statments made. . . .

Bread for the World never sought the endorsement of Lucis Trust and was not aware of its existence. We do not believe that an unsolicited endorsement should be the basis upon which we are held suspect.

On page 162 you state that "Bread for the World has not bought a grain of rice for anyone." That is absolutely right, but neither have we claimed to have done so. We are an interdenominational Christian citizens' movement against hunger. We do not seek to compete with or replace the work of relief groups. Instead we seek to complement their work by advocating public policies that prevent hunger. . . .

Also on page 162 it is stated that we have lobbied for "creation of global reserves and agencies to control the distribution of world assets." We know of no specific agency that controls the distribution of world assets. This statement is incorrect and needs qualification. . . .

In the Bread for the World statement of policy enclosed, we advocate "nationally held grain reserves" rather than world grain reserves. We believe these reserves held by each country to prevent famine are more effective and feasible.[4]

Cumbey's observations fail to see distinctions among liberal, evangelical, and fundamental American Christianity. She appears genuinely shocked and surprised that liberal denominations (United Methodist, Presbyterian U.S.A., Episcopal, etc.) are apparently promoting New Age and non-Christian practices and teachings. However, evangelicals by definition are not active participants in liberalism and so would not assume that what is happening at their neighborhood Methodist church is a direct threat to them in their own fellowship. It is unfair to take Bread for the World, an organization which promotes itself as interdenominational, and try to cram it into a fundamentalist mold, only to then accuse it of not fitting.[5]

Each Christian who considers supporting or endorsing Bread for the World needs to investigate carefully its structure, agenda, and correspondence and compare it with the biblical view of charity. However, such investigations should not be done with witch hunting techniques.

COALITION ON REVIVAL

The Coalition on Revival has been accused of promoting Christian militarism and of being a front organization for the New Age Movement and/or quasi-Christian aberrations.

The Background

The Coalition on Revival (COR) first convened in August 1984 in Denver, Colorado. Dozens of Christian leaders from all segments of American evangelicalism gathered to form a body committed to revival in the Church in America. COR and its various committees and boards have met periodically since then, working on a design for Christian vision and leadership that can have an effect on American society. The founders of COR believed that the Christian Church could have an appreciable impact on American society if Christians would stop fighting among themselves, be unified in common belief and goal, and have a commitment to proclaiming the gospel in and through every segment of their lives. Each COR member pledged to uphold orthodox, evangelical Christianity; to promote biblical ethics and perspectives in all areas of private and public life; and to pray actively for revival in America. Through networking, awareness raising, publication, and discussion, COR members hoped to overturn what they saw as a dangerous malaise within the Body of Christ.

The Coalition on Revival committees prepared documents outlining what they believed represent normative biblical views on all of the major areas of human thought and society. The completed documents are within the mainstream of evangelical activism with which many Christians agree.

The Charges

Some Christians, including some of the founding members who have resigned, are uncomfortable with what they perceive as COR's militancy. Some seem to believe that involvement in social or political arenas, even as the prophetic voice of Christian truth, invariably becomes a "slippery slope" down which good Christians slide to eventual wild-eyed, fanatical, revolutionary "Christian militarism."

To see what religious entanglement with society gets you, some reason, look at Iran. Replace a nice, middle-of-the-road Shah with a religious fundamentalist ayatolla, and end up with religious tyranny, civil war, and terrorism. Better for the Church to stick with preaching the gospel and leave the legislative process to the pagans. Actually, neither COR nor this view deals with the question, "Is government, by nature, always corrupting? Or does corruption in government become self-fulfilling prophecy when the noncorrupt refuse to serve in it?"

There have been many critics of COR, and some criticisms are well taken.[6] But the three critics we cite here are ones whose accusations fall into witch hunting rather than biblical judgment.

Dave Hunt's Criticisms

Dave Hunt barely mentioned COR in *Beyond Seduction,* but references to COR pepper *Whatever Happened to Heaven?* and COR is also prominently mentioned in several of his newsletters.[7] What he has written combines a number of witch hunting techniques. He switches terminology about COR, implying that COR substitutes law for grace; rejects COR because he perceives its eschatology as different from his; and commits the similar-equals-same fallacy, linking COR to the New Age Movement because of similar goals.

> Closely related in belief are several other groups; . . . whose major focus is upon cleaning up the earth ecologically, politically, economically, sociologically, etc. They imagine that the main function of the Church is to restore the Edenic state—hardly helpful, since Eden is where sin began. Many groups are beginning to work together who disagree on some points but share with the New Agers a desire to clean up earth and establish the Kingdom. I expect such cooperative efforts to grow, even involving Christian leaders who are not aware of what they are actually promoting. One example is the Coalition on Revival that in-

cludes . . . evangelical stalwarts . . . who are not aware that the actual intention of the leaders of COR falls in line with what we are discussing.[8]

In *Whatever Happened to Heaven?* Hunt was much more sweeping in his denouncement of COR:

Unfortunately, in spite of its prestigious leadership, COR's agenda fosters an unbiblical earthly mindedness which is contrary to that which Christ encouraged and which characterized the early church.[9]

In defiance both of logic and Scripture, COR's *Manifesto* declares that the Great Commission enjoins the church, as "the world's teacher, example, salt, light," to persuade secular societies and their institutions to adopt a Christian lifestyle.[10]

Grimstead makes an unbiblical and unreasonable connection between the church and the world from which it is supposed to be separate, and perverts the Great Commission in the process. Far from imposing biblical morality upon the unsaved, the Bible warns that attempting to keep the law will not save and will only breed self-righteousness. It is, moreover, an impossible standard for the non-Christian.[11]

The COR *Manifesto* echoes: "When Jesus returns, He will gain no greater authority over this earth and the forces of Satan than He had from the moment He ascended to and sat upon His throne. . . ." Though true, such a declaration is made to promote the false impression that what happens in the world depends only upon God's power.[12]

The most troubling feature of the COR and Reconstructionist agenda is that they are designed to create a world not only of Nicodemuses but of Pharisees of the worst sort. In their zeal to bring both the world and the church back under the Law, they do violence to grace and pervert the Great Commission. Our fears that the gospel of salvation of individuals will take second place to the desire to impose a superficial morality upon society would seem to be justified.[13]

Georgie Kinyon is the director of We Care Ministries, a central California counter-cult ministry specializing in helping people who have damaged their biblical faith through involvement in Christian fringe movements. She deals especially with casualties due to excesses within the charismatic movement.

Among other things, she links COR to "the Moonies, the Shepherding Movement . . . and various Faith leaders, such as Kenneth Copeland."[14] This is how she responded to the articles of the COR *Manifesto,* the foundational document signed by all COR participants:

> I agreed with everything until I came to 7. Lordship of Christ Non-optional; 11. Christian maturity. This could be used as a weapon by those within the Shepherding Movement to lord it over God's flock; 12. The Necessity of human accountability. This too could be used to place Christians into bondage. My question is, Who would be placing who into leadership, and by what authority? 13. The Need for Confrontation: dealing with church discipline. This too could be used as a tool of Satan to keep Christians into bondage by the Shepherding Movement; 16. Humility Required. This is also a form of shepherding. . . .[15]

Pauline MacPherson published several reports on COR through her Bold Truth Press. She charged COR participants with "entering this binding covenant relationship and indoctrination into a 'New View of Christianity.'"[16] She declared,

Underneath this "New move of God" or the "fresh Word from God" is the old Discipleship and Submission to Authority Movement. The body of Christ has been brainwashed by Bob Mumford. . . .

This is not a "New Move of God" or a "fresh Word of God." It is a resurrected form of government by ecclesiastical rulers—dominion of hierarchy officials in successive ranks or orders.[17]

These various criticisms of COR can be summarized under the following basic points: (1) collusion with the New Age Movement; (2) unbiblical earthly mindedness; (3) perversion of the Great Commission; (4) promotion of the law which kills rather than grace which brings life; (5) links with the Moonies and positive confession leaders; and (6) collusion with the Shepherding Movement.

The Evaluation

We have talked with many of the individuals involved in COR, read many of their documents and publications, talked with people who have resigned from COR, and kept up-to-date on current COR activities. Bob attended the initial convention in Denver, but neither of us are members of COR. To consolidate our report, we have quoted extensively from Cal Beisner, a member of COR's Executive Committee, one of COR's founders, assistant to the COR document general editor, and Gretchen's brother.[18] Cal is author of *God in Three Persons, Prosperity and Poverty,* and *Psalms of Promise.*

Beisner describes COR's structure:

First, we have a Steering Committee consisting of nearly 100 Christian leaders from various professions and various locations all around the country.

. . . All of these men stand firmly within the bounds of historic, orthodox Christianity—as indeed they and all members of the Steering Committee must in order to sign our doctrinal statement. . . . Our goal is to work together because of our unity in the one Body of Christ, finding strength in our mutual commitments to the most essential elements of the evangelical faith. The result has been a depth of cooperation beyond anything I've ever seen before, and a spirit of love for which I praise God time and again whenever we get together. We see ourselves as fighting a great battle—for the salvation of souls, for the building up of the saints, and for the changing of the world in every respect.[19]

The Charge of New Age Collusion

By now you should be experienced at identifying witch hunting techniques, especially when they are logical fallacies. COR can not be indicted as a New Age conspirator simply because some of its goals or activities are similar to New Age goals and activities. By this fallacious standard, we were able to turn the Bible, God's Word, into a New Age Handbook in Chapter 6. After all, the Bible promotes a new world order (Rev. 21:1–4), has a global network (Matt. 28:19), promotes a one world leader (Tit. 2:13), and promotes world ecological control (Gen. 1:26,28).

Perhaps it is not *what* COR promotes that bothers Hunt and/or Kinyon nearly as much as *when* COR thinks these goals can be reached. That, then, becomes a problem of eschatology, not of collusion. But that brings us new witch hunting problems.

First, as we have already seen, it is *essential* to believe that Jesus Christ is coming back physically and that God will ultimately and finally triumph over evil. But neither the Church nor the Scriptures excludes from orthodoxy those who disagree about *when* Christ will return or *how* God's triumph will be instituted. In fact, out of 112 members of the Steering Committee of COR, nine are postmillennial, two are amillennial, and 101 are premillennial (like Hunt, although not all 101 are necessarily pretribulational).

Second, Hunt has also presented no evidence to show that COR's position is that its goals can be fully realized, only that Christians ought to work toward those goals. In fact, Beisner notes,

> What we do believe, though, is that a full understanding of the clause in the Lord's Prayer, "Thy will be done, on earth as it is in heaven," requires that our actions back up our words. We don't know the *extent* to which God's will can be done on earth as it is in heaven prior to the return of Christ. But to whatever extent we can help make it so, we're committed to giving it our best try. And we believe premillennialists, amillennialists, and postmillennialists alike can agree to that and work together on that basis.[20]

If it is a chargeable offense for Christians to believe or practice anything any particular nonbeliever believes or practices, then Hunt would have a point. Then similar *would* prove same. But we have already seen that similar is *not* same. If it were, then we should stop believing in the inerrancy of God's Word because we will be similar to Jehovah's Witnesses, who also believe in the inerrancy of God's Word (but not, of course, in the Trinity, the deity of Christ, salvation by grace, etc.). We should stop believing that murder is wrong, because many secular humanists use a relativistic ethic to argue against murder. Whatever COR's flaws might be, collusion with the New Age Movement has not been proved.

The Charge of Earthly Mindedness

Related to the unease some pretribulationists have with COR's activisim is Hunt's charge that COR is guilty of "unbiblical earthly mindedness" and "unbiblical and unreasonable connection between the church and the world." From the context of Hunt's quotes it is apparent that Hunt sees COR's activism as unbiblical and unreasonable because, according to Hunt's eschatology, it is doomed to failure. This skirts very close to the edge of utilitarian ethics, that is, an action's goodness or badness depends on its results.

For example, the utilitarian says that an attempt to save a drowning victim that fails is not as good as an attempt that succeeds. By contrast, the biblical ethicist says that attempting to save a drowning victim is in itself good, whether or not it is successful. Jesus said that the poor would always be with us (Matt. 26:11), but he still commanded us to help the poor (Luke 18:22).

From the same perspective, Christian activists (regardless of their eschatological positions) understand their activism as good even if it is doomed to failure, short of God's direct intervention at the end of the Age.[21]

For Hunt to prove his charge, he would have to do more than show that his interpretation of eschatology is correct. Hunt does believe that a certain amount of activism is biblically permissible:

> Of course, the distinction must be made between trying to force values upon others, and simply standing true to personal convictions in obedience to God. It is one thing to protect our own children from godless influences that are an offense to God and that violate the charge He has given to governments. It is some-

thing else to attempt to force biblical values on a godless world. For example, it may not be necessary to
change the curriculum in order to prevent our own
children from being adversely affected. The protest or
action ought to provide an appropriate remedy (such
as exempting the children of Christian parents from
certain instructions) rather than attempting to force
Christian values upon the population at large.[22]

He goes on to say that elected office is even an option for Christians, although "The higher the level of
government . . . the less likely it is that the elected
official can function as a Christian."[23] By limited activism, but criticism of COR, does Hunt mean that it
is all right to get involved, but only if you do not try
to do very much, and only if you do not expect to be
successful? Is care for our own children acceptable
but concern for others earthly minded? Is mediocre
activism okay but fervent activism unbiblical?

To show COR guilty of "unbiblical earthly mindedness" Hunt would have to show that COR's activism is *instead of* or *more important than* preaching the gospel. He has not shown that.

The Charge of Perversion of the Great Commission

This charge is an example of the false alternative
witch hunting technique. It is assumed that *inclusion* of social and/or political activism within the
Great Commission (Matt. 28:19–20) means *exclusion* of evangelism. However, this is not necessarily
so. Instead of making a false alternative of either activism or evangelism, Christian activists, including
COR members, see it as both activism and evangelism.

To make this a valid charge, critics would have to
prove that the passage itself excludes activism, even

that activism which is one of the vehicles of evangelism described elsewhere (Matt. 26:31–46). This they have not done.

The Charge of Law Rather Than Grace

This charge comes from a "crossed-wires" confusion between actions and goals. The argument goes like this: Grace saves people. Law does not. COR promotes law, even over nonbelievers. Therefore, COR tries to save people by law. COR is wrong.

However, this is a misunderstanding of the dynamics of grace and law. The first two premises are true: grace saves people; law does not. But the Bible says that law has two functions: to reveal to us our sinfulness (Rom. 7:7; Gal. 3:24); *and* to restrain our sinful acts (Rom. 13:3–4; Gal. 3:23). In fact, 1 Timothy 1:8–10 declares:

> But we know that the law is good if one uses it lawfully, knowing this: that the law is not made for a righteous person, but for the lawless and insubordinate, for the ungodly and for sinners, for the unholy and profane, for murderers of fathers and murderers of mothers, for manslayers, for fornicators, for sodomites, for kidnappers, for liars, for perjurers, and if there is any other thing that is contrary to sound doctrine.

If COR, or any other organization claiming to be Christian, were to emphasize law as a way of *salvation,* they would be heretical. But to promote law in its rightful, biblical place is not heretical. Nowhere does COR literature promote its activism or goals of legislative reform as vehicles of salvation. The charge is invalid. One cannot base his rejection of those who claim to be Christians on the basis of a *fear* "that the gospel of salvation of individuals will take second place to the desire to impose a superficial morality upon society."[24]

The Charge of Moonie and
Positive Confession Link

Often cult apologetics organizations cannot keep current on all of the groups and individuals about whom they are questioned. There are literally thousands of cultic and occultic groups in the United States alone, some with only a handful of members, others, like the Mormons, with millions of members. It is even harder to keep current on the thousands of organizations and churches that are not heretical, but which are controversial. However, if we make public pronouncements or publish on any group or individual, our integrity should compel us to comprehensive, accurate, and up-to-date research. It is especially easy to slip into witch hunting by stopping short of responsible research.

Georgie Kinyon's linking of COR to the Unification Church cult (the Moonies) gave the impression that COR compromised with cultism; there can be no compromise between orthodoxy and heresy.

However, Kinyon did not present the full story behind the rumor. One individual with questionable Moonie ties was once a member of COR. Bob Grant now directs Christian Voice in Washington, D.C., which was once Christian right activist Colonel Doner's headquarters. When the COR Executive Committee was told of Grant's possible affiliation with the Moonies, they requested from Grant evidence to the contrary. Because Grant could not satisfy COR that he and his work were totally disassociated with the Unification Church and received no funding from them, he was removed from membership. Far from proving Moonie involvement in COR, this proves just the opposite: when Moonie influence was perceived, it was removed. Beisner notes:

> Because of these similar [anti-Communist, free enterprise, conservative] goals, there may be some similar items on the political agendas of the Moonies and COR—but those similar agendas are because of similar goals, not because of any influence of one group on the other. COR emphatically, categorically, unquestioningly, univocally, and totally rejects Moon's theology. It is absolutely committed to historic, evangelical Christian theology.[25]

As to the link between COR and positive confession, even the critics agree that the most prominent positive confession teachers such as Kenneth Copeland, Fred Price, Paul Yonggi Cho, and Kenneth Hagin are not involved in COR. The strongest link that can be made is that of guilt by association. Because some COR people are sometimes associated with some positive confession people, COR must be influenced by positive confession. Witch hunting does not prove links.

The Charge of Shepherding

According to some critics, COR president Jay Grimstead is controlled by his "shepherd," Dennis Peacocke, who is also a member of the COR Executive Committee. With power through Grimstead and Peacocke, it is supposed, COR has become little more than the private agenda maker of the unbiblical and oppressive Shepherding movement. It is not our purpose here to evaluate the Shepherding Movement, its changes over the years, or its current status and leadership.[26]

However, it is witch hunting to attribute unbiblical actions to an organization and all of its members on the basis of suspicion rather than proof. If a shepherding conspiracy exists in COR, it violates all available evidence. Responsible discernment never accuses or convicts without evidence. Article Twelve of the COR document on pastoral renewal states,

> We affirm that pastoral authority is limited by Scripture to those areas of life on which Scripture clearly speaks, and that outside those areas pastors ought humbly to give wise counsel without insisting on strict obedience as a condition of continued fellowship or shepherding (Rom. 14).

> We deny that pastoral authority ever entails a duty on the part of laymen to disobey God's laws in deference to pastors, to accept all pastoral counsel outside the clear revelations of Scripture, or to break down proper Biblical authority structures within family, church, and society.[27]

We are not saying that there *could not* exist abuses of power or shepherding influences in COR or any other Christian organization. But focus on the witch hunting technique used here. "Lordship of Christ," "Christian maturity," "Necessity of human accountability," "Need for confrontation," and "Humility required" are phrases Kinyon is convinced prove the shepherding power in COR. But anyone who reads the articles under each phrase can see that they are not referring to or allowing for shepherding. Responsible, non-shepherding, biblical Christians can use each of those phrases in contexts well within orthodox Christian practice. The titles of the articles and the articles themselves could be *abused* to promote shepherding. But so can the Scriptures themselves. We cannot indict the Scriptures because heretics abuse them. Rather than proving her suspicion, Kinyon has used witch hunting to indict an organization whose official stance is against that of which she is accusing it.

Summary

Witch hunting against the Coalition on Revival falls into the patterns outlined in the early part of this book. You are now well versed in recognizing techniques like "guilt by association," "term switching," and "vague definition." You can see how comprehensive, up-to-date research is vital for fair representation.

Biblical discernment is a serious business, and those who accept the challenge to engage in warfare with the enemy must be sure they are using weapons in the right way against the right targets. Fair criticism rebukes the sinner and strengthens the Church. Unfair criticism changes the excellency of our calling into mediocrity.

RECONSTRUCTIONISM

The reconstructionists have been accused of many things, including anti-Semitism, substituting law for grace, political militancy, collusion with New Ageism, and collusion with the Antichrist.

The Background

Postmillennialism, in simple terms, is the eschatological (end times) view asserting that there is a period of worldwide biblical influence and authority, during which a greater percentage of the population comes to salvation than during any other time, all of which will culminate in the visible second coming of Jesus Christ. The postmillennialists do not see the millennium as a literal thousand-year period of time, and they do not interpret the prophetic Scriptures to include a rapture of the Church, either pre-, mid-, or posttribulation. How and in what manner this biblical influence and authority spreads and the extent to which it permeates society are explained differently by various postmillennialists.

One way in which postmillennialism differs from dispensational premillennialism is that postmillennialism believes that it is possible for the Church, empowered by the Holy Spirit, to be used by God to institute the society that the premillennialists believe can only be brought in through direct intervention after Jesus' second coming. Postmillennialists are *optimistic* in the sense that they see a continuum between the Holy Spirit in the Church and the power of God in society. Premillennialists are *pessimistic* in the sense that they see a sharp demarcation between the Holy Spirit in the Church and the power of God in society. Both, of course, are *optimistic* in the sense that they have absolute faith in God's power to accomplish his will, with or without the Church.

Postmillennial *reconstructionism* is a term recently popular which describes the cumulative influence of individual regeneration on society. Reconstructionists affirm that this Christian influence is initiated by the preaching of the gospel and the transformation of individuals through the call and power of the Holy Spirit in conviction, regeneration, and sanctification. Reconstructionist Gary DeMar stated that they "are not revolutionary because they believe that Christians achieve leadership by living righteously. Dominion is by ethical service and work, not by revolution."[28]

There have been devoted Christians through the ages who have been pre-, a-, or postmillennial. One of the most prominent postmillennialists of the last century was Charles Hodge. His *Systematic Theology* is a classic and a standard text in many Bible colleges and seminaries. Other classic postmillennial theologians include the champion of biblical inspiration, B. B. Warfield, and defender of biblical doctrine, J. G. Machen. Contemporary postmillennialists[29] in America include R. J. Rushdoony, Gary North, David Chilton, Greg Bahnsen, and others.

The Charges

We will examine four different representative sources of accusations against postmillennial reconstructionism:[30] Hal Lindsey's *The Road to Holocaust;*[31] Ray Nelson's article "Whose Kingdom Come . . . ?"[32] Constance Cumbey's radio interview on the Lou Davies' Show;[33] and Dave Hunt's *Whatever Happened to Heaven?*[34]

Hal Lindsey

Hal Lindsey wrote *The Road to Holocaust* to warn the Church about what he considers to be the most potentially anti-Semitic movement since Hitler: the reconstructionists.[35] The back cover of the book warns, "Let Christians not sit idly by while a system of prophetic interpretation that historically furnished the philosophical basis for anti-Semitism infects the Church again."[36]

Lindsey sees the post- and amillennial positions as inherently susceptible to anti-Semitism because, unlike Lindsey's brand of dispensational pretribulationalism, the two former positions do not believe in a special future prophetic role for national Israel. He comments,

> However, from the standpoint of anti-Semitism, both Postmils and Amils are equally guilty of creating a climate of thought wherein the Jew is viewed as an obstinate and rebellious pretender to the covenants and promises that are now exclusively owned by the Church. Since in this view the Jew has no more special purpose in God's plan as a national people, they see no reason for them to exist as a distinct people or as a modern state. . . . Historically, these factors created the kind of soil in which anti-Semitism easily took root and sprang to life.[37]

Lindsey has no tolerance for post- or amillennial interpretations of prophetic Scripture. He accuses the reconstructionists of manipulating Scripture, a sin so serious he calls it blasphemous:

> The Dominionists try to explain this away by saying that Israel's sin of rejecting the Messiah made all of these promises null and void. To me, this kind of teaching blasphemes the character of God.[38]

Lindsey warns that the reconstructionists are the first step to genocide for the Jews, as he says the German Church was before Hitler's genocide of the Jews:

> However, the Dominionists, who proclaim that the Church is now Israel and that the descendants of Abraham, Isaac, and Jacob have no future hope as a distinct people, are finding a very wary eye cast their way. The Jews have heard this kind of rhetoric from the Church before. They remember vividly the anti-Semitism and persecutions it inevitably set in mo-

tion. They remember well the historic progression: The Church said "You have no right to live among us as Jews!" The secular governments followed with "You have no right to live among us!" The Nazis concluded with "You have no right to live!"[39]

On the other hand, Lindsey is quick to laud the efforts of his fellow dispensationalists, who reassure the Jews with their "true" understanding of Scripture:

It takes a demonstration of genuine love as well as the Gospel to overcome the effects of those so-called Christians in past history who believed that the Church was God's theocratic kingdom on earth, and in its name sought either to convert the Jews or eliminate them.[40]

Another charge against the reconstructionists by Lindsey is similar to Hunt's charge of earthly-mindedness against COR:

This kind of teaching has made the Dominionists "so earthly-minded that they are no heavenly good." . . . they often seem to be more interested in political takeover than evangelizing and discipling people for a spiritual kingdom. In some ways they are coming dangerously close to fulfilling Peter's prediction [mockers full of lust from 2 Peter 3:3–6].[41]

The Road to Holocaust is a diatribe against reconstructionism. Lindsey is not offering a critique of an alternate eschatology or a criticism of a diversity within the Body of Christ. He categorizes them with those who are anti-Semitic, blasphemous, and mockers of God's Word, full of lust.[42] Such charges against those who claim to be Christian brothers should never be made without fidelity to Scripture, impeccable reasoning, and ironclad evidence.

Ray Nelson

Passport, published by Calvary Chapel of West Covina, takes a strong dispensational and also charismatic stand in harmony with the other Calvary Chapels and with the teachings of the original Calvary Chapel of Costa Mesa pastor, Chuck Smith. Article author Ray Nelson is concerned about what he sees as reconstructionism's "law over grace" heresy:

> It is in this area of law vs. grace that Kingdom theology proponents are on heretical ground: through their adherence to the Law, they deny the grace of God through His work on the cross. . . .
>
> The Bible is clear, however, that the Church in the last days would be one possessing only a little power and that any work to be done would be done by Jesus Christ Himself through the Church, and that the Church would be rescued, by Jesus, "from the hour of temptation, which shall come upon the world, to try them that dwell upon the earth" (Rev. 3:7–13). . . .
>
> Kingdom Now or Dominionist theology is dangerous to the Christian Church because of its heresy of distorting and denying the Gospel of Jesus Christ. It is dangerous to all of society because it promises a state church dictatorship.[43]

Constance Cumbey

Constance Cumbey goes as far as Lindsey in saying that the reconstructionists are dupes or agents of the Antichrist. Here is what she had to say on postmillennial reconstructionism during a radio interview:

[Interviewer: Is it postmillennialism in general or their brand of it that bothers you?]

It's postmillennialism in general. I think it's totally unscriptural, I think it's part of the final deception. You have to throw out huge chunks of Scripture to subscribe to postmillennialism. . . . And Rushdoony's logic sounds remarkably like the *Humanist Manifesto*. Now, I don't think Rushdoony's a humanist himself. Far from it, I think the man does fear and trust God, but I think that he has intellectually absorbed these people's arguments, he has not gone behind to see where these people were coming from. Some of the people he's quoting are people . . . who are active in humanist and New Age circles both, some of the names that did sign the *Humanist Manifesto*. And he's absorbing it, and he's basing his arguments more on that than on Scripture.[44]

Dave Hunt

Dave Hunt's *Beyond Seduction* was one of the first contemporary books linking reconstructionism with heresy.[45] In *Beyond Seduction* he linked them with the heresies of the Manifested Sons of God movement. In summarizing his criticisms he dichotomized between preaching the gospel and meeting temporal needs:

The focus is turned from heaven to this earth, from a new universe that only God can create to a new world that we hope to fashion by our own efforts. It is just one more form of the selfism that plagues society and the church, another way of becoming little gods, of turning from Him to ourselves by assuming a responsibility to do what only He can do.[46]

Hunt spoke more freely in his *Christian Information Bureau Bulletin* where he stated, "If the real

Jesus Christ is going to catch His bride up from earth to meet Him *in the air* (1 Thess. 4:17), then those who work to build a kingdom for a 'Christ' whom they will meet with their feet planted on earth have been under heavy delusion indeed! They have been working for the Antichrist!"[47]

Criticism of reconstructionism[48] abounds in *Whatever Happened to Heaven?* in which Hunt has almost hopelessly tangled reconstructionism, COR, and dominionism, assuming that what is said or believed by one is accepted by all. Representative witch hunting remarks follow.

Concerning efforts to influence society and the world:

Not only have all such efforts [to "Christianize" society] failed to produce a sustained increase in general piety, but the end result has invariably been detrimental for the secular world as well as for the church.[49]

Concerning Christian political activism:

It would be a complete contradiction, then, for those who are united with Christ in His crucifixion and rejection by the world, to compromise their Christianity by getting voted in by Christ-rejecters to high office in order to help run this world in partnership with those who despise their Lord.[50]

Concerning law vs. grace and forceful domination of society:

The Reconstructionists such as Rushdoony and North . . . are the same kind of legalists whom Paul refuted in the Galatian epistle. They hope to enforce upon both the church and an unconverted world laws given to Israel as God's peculiar people, but which neither Israel nor any other unregenerate people could keep.[51]

Zealous Christians sincerely believe they are supposed to dominate non-Christians in the process of taking dominion over cultures and nations. It is not surprising, then, that the non-Christians feel threatened by the determination of these dominionists to force their beliefs upon the rest of society.[52]

Concerning Hunt's interpretation of the reformed (Calvinist) view of predestination, to which genuine reconstructionists (postmillennial, reformed reconstructionists—not charismatic, premillennial dominionists or Kingdom Now advocates) generally subscribe:

While some verses which present predestination could possibly be given a Calvinistic interpretation, to do so would contradict the remainder of Scripture and therefore must not be done.

. . . Yet in spite of such Scriptures and His command to us to love our enemies and to be Good Samaritans to all who need our help, God Himself, according to Calvinism, has chosen not to save billions from hell even though, through extending His irresistible grace, He could do so. This is both a libel on God's character and such a contradiction of Scripture that it must be rejected vehemently.[53]

It would be a libel upon God's character (as well as a denial of the clear teaching of many Scriptures), to say that He is able, but unwilling, to save all.[54]

The Evaluation

With so many quotations from so many authors on so many subjects, it is easy to lose sight of this book's focus: witch hunting techniques and how to avoid them. Whole books can, have been, and will continue to be written on reconstructionism, Calvinism, eschatology, and activism. But in this book we need to refocus attention on witch hunting, our main theme. Leaving aside the above authors' debatable representations of reconstructionism, Calvinism, eschatology, and activism,[55] let us examine the witch hunting techniques these quotes illustrate.

The Charge of Anti-Semitism

Earlier in this book we quoted the noted scholar of American religions, J. Gordon Melton, on the seriousness of charging anyone with Nazi anti-Semitism: "Given the present situation, living as we do in a post-Holocaust world, such ascription is more than a minor error, it is serious slander."[56] This is not an honest disagreement on the theological interpretation of a belief within Christianity. It is a charge which, if true, excludes the reconstructionists from the Body of Christ. Lindsey's caveats about reconstructionists being well-meaning, ignorant, unsuspecting people who unintentionally allow for anti-Semitism ring hollow. Can one be a well-meaning blasphemer?

Lindsey bases his charge of anti-Semitism on two points: (1) reconstructionists do not believe in a future special prophetic role for national Israel; and (2) any theology in history which has done this has been followed by periods of anti-Semitism.

First, does it logically follow that denial of a future special prophetic role for Israel allows for anti-Semitism? Here Lindsey unfortunately slips into the witch hunting technique of the false alternative. That is, he assumes that one either agrees with the dispensationalist that Israel has a special place or one is vulnerable to anti-Semitism. However, he has failed to consider that there could be reasons *other than* a prophetic role for Israel that could restrain anti-Semitism.

One reconstructionist confessed to us that, if denying Israel a prophetic role was anti-Semitic, then he guessed he must be anti-Italian and anti-Greek too. Of course, he was being facetious, but his humor illustrates our point. A people or nation does not have to be prophetically *special* in order to be *equal*. In fact, nondispensationalists of whatever age have been constrained from anti-Semitism because of the clear commands of Scripture, epitomized so completely in the story of the Good Samaritan (Luke 10:30–37).

> If it is possible, as much as depends on you, live peaceably with all men (Rom. 12:18).

> Therefore, as we have opportunity, let us do good to all, especially to those who are of the household of faith (Gal. 6:10).

> Therefore, whatever you want men to do to you, do also to them, for this is the Law and the Prophets (Matt. 7:12).

> And the second [commandment] is like it: "You shall love your neighbor as yourself" (Matt. 22:39).

Lindsey does an injustice to the reconstructionists to assume that their eschatology would cause them to echo, "You have no right to live among us as Jews." Lack of "favored-nation" status does not automatically mean "illegitimate-nation" status. If the only thing restraining Christians from persecuting the Jews is dispensationalism, then why aren't dispensationalists and all other Christians persecuting Ethiopians, Guatemalans, and members of all other nations not protected by dispensational prophetic interpretation? The reconstructionists do not want to "convert the Jews or eliminate them" any more than they or any other Christians want to "convert or eliminate" any group or individual. After all, the reconstructionists know that it is God who "has made from one blood every nation of men to dwell on all the face of the earth, and has determined their pre-appointed times and the boundaries of their habitation" (Acts 17:26).

In fact, a reconstructionist interpretation of Romans 11:26 is that the body of Jews *will* be converted, before the second coming of Christ. Reconstructionists point out, however, that "post-millennialism denies . . . that the Jews can be members of God's people apart from their conversion to the Messiah. The Jews will be saved, the postmillennialist teaches, only by faith in Christ, repentance, and entrance into the life of the Body of Christ."[57]

Second, by saying that every historical period of theological non-favored-nation-in-prophecy-status-for-Israel is followed by persecution of the Jews does *not* prove that the theology *produced* the persecution. This is called a "false cause" fallacy in logic. That is, sequence of events does not prove cause of events. For example, roosters crow before the sun comes up. Does that mean that the roosters' crowing makes the sun come up?

Let's turn the principle on Lindsey to show that it is an invalid way to argue. Lindsey and most dispensationalists will say that dispensational pretribulational premillennialism has never been so popular nor so thoroughly developed as in the last two hundred years. But that last two hundred years has also seen the most large-scale persecutions and, in fact, the very Holocaust of the Jews which Lindsey tries to lay at the feet of postmillennialists. But the fact that the rise of dispensationalism precedes the rise in persecutions and the ultimate anti-Semitism does not mean that dispensationalism *produced* or provided the *basis for* persecution and anti-Semitism. To prove a causal connection between post-millennialism and anti-Semitism, Lindsey would have to prove that postmillennialism is inherently anti-Semitic, or that it intrinsically allows for anti-Semitism on the basis of its theological content. This he has not done.

The Charges of Blasphemy, Mockery, and Libel

Blasphemy is defined as "cursing God." *Mockery* is to imitate in derision or fun. *Libel,* the written version of slander, is a statement that unjustly damages a person's reputation.

The Bible tells us that blasphemy arises out of pride (Ps. 73:9,11), hatred (Ps. 74:18), defiance (Isa. 36:15–20), and self-deification (Dan. 11:36–37; 2 Thess. 2:4).

Mockery comes from fools (Prov. 14:9) and Jude describes mockers in the last times as those "who would walk according to their own ungodly lusts. These are sensual persons, who cause divisions, not having the Spirit" (v. 18).

Scripture condemns slander, describing it as destructive (Prov. 11:9), deceitful (Ps. 52:2), deluding (Prov. 10:18), and devouring (Prov. 16:27–30). The devil (Job 1:9–11), revilers (1 Pet. 3:16), hypocrites (Prov. 11:9), and false leaders (3 John 9–10) are all slanderers. In fact, Paul warns Christians that malicious gossiping (libel or slander) characterizes non-believers, not Christians (Titus 3:1–3).

By calling reconstructionists, postmillennialists, and Calvinists, blasphemers, mockers, and libelers, Lindsey and Hunt are, in effect, excluding them from the Body of Christ. Do they have warrant for such judgment?

Not at all. Lindsey says they blasphcmc for cquating Israel with the Church. Since when has that interpretation of eschatology been a test for orthodoxy? Is Lindsey willing to accuse Augustine, Luther, Calvin, Warfield, and Murray (each of whom he elsewhere acknowledges as Christians, sometimes even praising their Christianity of blasphemy)?

Lindsey feels justified in pairing reconstructionists with mockers of God, full of lust (2 Pet. 3:3–6) because they seem to him to be more earthly minded than heavenly minded—not that they ignore or deny spiritual salvation and heaven, he notes, but that they do not emphasize it as much as he thinks they should. Is he willing to accuse Christian leaders such as Luther, Wilberforce, or William Jennings Bryan as mockers of God who are full of lust?

Hunt equates Calvinism with libel (or slander) of God because he believes Calvinism's predestination makes God unjust. Yet, as many Calvinist theologians have pointed out over the centuries, if all men sinned and are thus *deserving* of death, then God's election by grace of some but not all cannot be unjust. The argument goes, if a judge sentences five murderers to death but gives a stay of execution to one, he is only guilty of grace, not of injustice. Would Hunt accuse Hodgc, Warfield, or Machen of slander because of their Calvinism? Each of these was a champion of orthodoxy in the midst of the rise of liberalism.

The inconsistency of these charges is obvious. Witch hunting typically rejects those with whom we disagree, even when those disagreements are on debatable issues or within the framework of biblical orthodoxy. We can disagree with, argue with, and criticize other believers with whom we disagree on nonessential doctrines or interpretations of doctrines. But Scripture does not allow us to condemn except in matters of essential belief.

The Charge of Law over Gospel

Several critics accused reconstructionism of depending on law rather than gospel, or, as Nelson put it, the "heresy of distorting and denying the Gospel of Jesus Christ. . . . [is] dangerous to all of society because it promises a state church dictatorship." And Hunt is convinced that this desire to institute biblical law on the earth is a kind of idolatry, worship of the self, "another way of becoming little gods."

In order to substantiate these charges, the critics would have to produce evidence of more than what they term an *overemphasis* or *preoccupation* with law or even that such "Christianization" of society is not found or predicted in Scripture. Instead, the critics would have to produce evidence that reconstructionists *deny* salvation by grace or *affirm* salvation by works. Indeed, the average reader would infer from many of the critics' statements that they do assume the reconstructionists deny grace and affirm works.

But here's the witch hunting. Through a combination of faulty definitions and false analogy fallacies, the critics have managed to move the reconstructionist position from within orthodoxy to heresy. First, by broadening the category of "legalism heresy" to encompass *emphasizing* the law as well as *denying* grace. Second, by assuming that the only alternative to the dispensational dichotomy between law and grace is a heretical works righteousness. Over and over the critics assume that anyone who wants to institute biblical law in society is *substituting* that law for the gospel of salvation.

If the reconstructionists were really substituting law for grace, they would not be believers. However, even the reconstructionist quotes by the critics show instead that the reconstructionists' view of law is threefold: (1) to convict individuals of their sinfulness; (2) as a pattern for godly living by believers; and (3) as a way of restraining the sinful actions of the unregenerate. No reconstructionist says that law can ever save anyone at any time.[58] In fact, reconstructionists are in the Reformed tradition, after the great Reformers who broke with Roman Catholicism precisely because *they believed Rome taught salvation by the law, not by grace.* Witch hunting has confused the use of law *to order society* with grace *unto salvation.* It is not fair to condemn reconstructionists for teaching *salvation* by law when they are teaching *restrained lawlessness* by law.

The Charge of Antichrist Religion

Here is what the Bible has to say about the Antichrist and his religion: He is called the man of sin, the son of perdition (2 Thess. 2:3), the lawless one (2 Thess. 2:8), and the beast (Rev. 11:7). Antichrist is described as opposing God (2 Thess. 2:4), deceiving the world (2 John 7, Rev. 19:20), persecuting Christians (Rev. 13:7), Satan-inspired (2 Thess. 2:9), and denying Christ's incarnation (1 John 4:3; 2 John 7).

Linking reconstructionists to "the final deception" and "working for the Antichrist" is to deny their salvation. One cannot be lawless, deceitful, Satan-inspired, and denying Christ and yet belong to him.

By what evidence have the critics condemned the reconstructionists in this way? Cumbey says it is because they have similar goals to the New Age Movement and secular humanism. Hunt says it is because denying the Rapture and building an earthly Christian kingdom are the Antichrist's work.

But look at this carefully. Does similar prove same? Because reconstructionists look *similar* to New Agers and secular humanists, because they have some similar goals, does that make them the *same* as New Agers and secular humanists? Of course not. That's not evidence of Antichrist collusion, it's evidence of the witch hunting technique of confusing what is similar with what is the same. Are denial of the Rapture and building an earthly Christian kingdom denials of essential doctrine? Neither one denies the biblical doctrine of God, Jesus Christ, man, sin and salvation, or Scripture. *Essential* is that Christ is coming physically again. Rapture or no Rapture is a peripheral issue. *Essential* is that Jesus Christ is Lord over all. How that is worked out in any particular kingdom is a debatable topic.

The Charge of Activism-Produced Sinfulness

The last type of criticism considered here concerns the dubious value or success of Christian involvement in society. The general criticism is that the reconstructionists are attempting to do too much in society and expecting too much from society. Hunt calls it "assuming a responsibility to do what only He can do" and "enforc[ing] upon both the church and an unconverted world laws . . . which neither

Israel nor any other regnerate people could keep."
This is not seen as just a mistake, an unrealistic ex-
pectation, or a difference in Christian social ethics.
Such an emphasis *forces* Christian values and laws
on nonbelievers and *forces* further social degeneration over time.

Three witch hunting techniques arise concerning
this issue. First, critics have confused human *imple-
mentation* with human *power*. The reconstructionists are no more saying that they can build the
perfect society without God's sovereign will and
power than a dispensationalist would say that he
could get somebody saved by telling him the gospel
without God's sovereign will and power. Now, legitimate disagreement exists in the Church about
whether or not God's will and power are dedicated to
building a perfect society through the Church, but
that is completely different from saying that anyone
who is postmillennial has the hopeless task of building perfection without God.

Second, critics confuse both the method and the
justification for Christian values in a social com-
posite of believers and nonbelievers. The critics have
produced no evidence that the reconstructionists
plan to implement their Christian society by force,
either locally or universally. Perhaps the critics
overlook the reconstructionists' references to change
from the bottom up, through the society-permeating
influence of changed lives, because these critics are
convinced that it cannot be done, and therefore any
attempt would eventually die or degenerate into
force. The critics also miss, again, that the reconstructionists see a Christian society with Christian
ethics as a way to order society and promote godly
living among believers *rather than* as a way of salvation. Certainly, imposing one's values on another

does not make him saved. The adage remains true, "A man convinced against his will is of the same opinion still." But that does not negate the fact that we impose our values on others all the time—not in the name of salvation, but in the name of law and justice.

For example, if someone were attacking your young child with a butcher knife, you would have no compunction about intervening physically and stopping the attack even if you had to hurt the attacker to do it. You have imposed your value (innocent children should not be butchered) on another. But your immediate goal, even as a Christian, was not to *save* the attacker but to *defend* your child. Once your child is safe, because of your imposition of your value on the attacker, then you can visit the attacker in jail and preach the gospel to him—to bring him to *salvation*. Confusion of ideas and terms is no way to prove heresy.

Third, our familiar "false cause" fallacy has resurfaced. Because degenerate societies follow "Christianized" societies does not necessarily mean that the "Christianization" of society *caused* the subsequent degeneration. Remember, the rooster's crowing does not cause the sun to rise. We are also skating close to the edge of utilitarian ethics again. If it were biblical to attempt to Christianize a society, it would be right to attempt it even if that attempt failed. Argue all you like about whether or not it is right to attempt it, but do not argue that it cannot be right because the attempt fails.

Summary

In our survey of reconstructionism we have seen that, while it is a minority position within the Church, it does not deny any of the essential doctrines of Christianity and it can be defended against these witch hunting accusations. Criticism, debate, theological argumentation, and competing exegesis are proper ways to explore and challenge the differences among Christians concerning eschatology, sovereignty and free will, and activism. But witch hunting is no substitute for truth. Unfortunately, it is often far easier to condemn than to tolerate diversity (not heresy) within the Body of Christ.

WITCH HUNTING DISGUISES INTOLERANCE AS INTEGRITY

One of the main principles illustrated throughout this book is that witch hunting disguises intolerance as integrity. This is the heart of all bigotry. We can see this clearly when we think of forms of prejudice with which all Christians should disagree.

Those who discriminate against the Jewish people do not often make rash and openly bigoted statements like, "I just don't like people who look so different and don't believe what I believe." Instead they will attempt to justify their irrational prejudice with arguments that sound reasonable on the surface: "Jews are always looking for a way to make money off other people"; "Jews were so blind that they crucified Christ"; "Jews don't have the same racial integrity we have." To our post-World War II Christian ears, these statements sound horrible. But the people who make them think they are reasonable. Are the witch hunting techniques and accusations we have examined in this book any more reasonable? Having looked carefully behind the rhetoric to the logic, we say they are not.

Our final example of witch hunting against organizations will provide, in summary form, illustrations of the spiritual bigotry characteristic of witch hunting. We do not know any Christian who wants to be a spiritual bigot, and one of the best ways to avoid unconsciously promoting spiritual bigotry is to zealously guard against falling into witch hunting.

This example will give you the opportunity to apply the biblical judgment techniques you have learned in this book and to identify some of the witch hunting techniques we have already exposed.

WORLD VISION

The Charges

The following is a portion of what Constance Cumbey said in *The Hidden Dangers of the Rainbow* concerning World Vision, an international famine relief and development ministry headquartered in Southern California.

> Another example is found in Stanley Mooneyham, the ex-president of World Vision. Mooneyham has long enjoyed great prominence in the Christian world. Yet his book, *What Do You Say to a Hungry World?* advocates zero population growth. Mooneyham says:
>
>> Insist on open forum discussions on birth control, *abortion, artificial insemination, genetic control* and *death control* in your church or club program. *Some of these subjects, unfortunately, seem to be outside of the orbit of evangelical Christian concern.*
>
>> . . . Several countries around the world have legislated family size with frightening consequences. Often the result is forced sterilization, infanticide, and abortion. Families are even faced with imposed economic consequences for the birth of an extra child.
>
> Mooneyham, however, has no problem with these measures. . . .[59]

Cumbey went on to indict Mooneyham and World Vision for promoting occultic acupuncture, compromise with indigenous religions, joint projects with Hindu ashrams, and holistic ministry.[60]

In Cumbey's second book, *A Planned Deception,* she accused World Vision, among other things, of using New Age vocabulary, promoting an international food bank, quoting New Agers, promoting abortion, sterilization, and birth control, and endorsing New Agers.[61]

The Evaluation

By this time you should be able to use your biblical discernment training to identify witch hunting techniques and answer most of the charges against World Vision yourself. Take a few moments and review the charges.

In Chapter 6, for example, we examined the context in which Mooneyham made the statement that Christians should lead discussions concerning abortion, population control, and so on. Even from the portion Cumbey quoted we can see that Mooneyham is not *advocating* these measures: he is merely saying that Christians should be involved in discussing the issues. Ted Engstrom, successor to Mooneyham as president of World Vision said,

Stan Mooneyham's comments . . . challenged Christians to be aware of issues such as abortion and birth control—because they are subjects that non-Christians are dealing with, *without well-educated opposition from the Christian community.*[62]

In response to Cumbey's accusation of New Age involvement because of the use of the term *holistic,* Engstrom responded,

For instance, we use the word "holistic" to describe our overseas development work that integrates community assistance such as agriculture and water systems with an evangelistic effort. Yet Ms. Cumbey says "holistic" is a New Age word involving spiritism and the occult. From this sort of thing she is associating us with this movement.[63]

We checked on Cumbey's charge that World Vision cooperated with a Hindu ashram. We have friends who are indigenous Indians, serving now in the United States as Christian missionaries to Muslims. We asked them to check with their sources in India concerning the Nava Jeevan Seva Ashram. Their finding: the ashram is not Hindu at all. It is a *Christian* community in India, dedicated to communicating the gospel on an Indian-to-Indian basis. As our friends explained, "*Ashram* is an Indian term meaning a community of believers, in this case a community of *Christian* believers. Cannot Indians be Christians without having to abandon our own language in favor of Americanisms?" World Vision confirmed:

The group is not Hindu. It has an overriding purpose: a Christian spiritual enhancement of the local people. The development project itself has documented evangelistic components, including staff training in evangelism and child evangelism.[64]

The other charges against World Vision can be answered similarly.

SUMMARY

Even inadvertent spiritual bigotry has no place in the Body of Christ. In John 17:22–23 Jesus petitioned his Father, asking, "that they may be one just as We are one: I in them, and You in Me; that they may be made perfect in one, and that the world may know that You have sent Me, and have loved them as You have loved Me."

Unity *based upon doctrinal integrity* is an earmark of biblical Christianity. World Vision has not violated essential biblical doctrine and actively brings the gospel to a world dying without it. James challenged Christians, "Show me your faith without your works, and I will show you my faith by my works" (James 2:18). World Vision stands behind its program of well-rounded (dare we say it?) holistic evangelism:

> World Vision has worked hard to maintain that balance during its 36 years of international ministry; to provide healing for the body, soul and spirit the way Christ did. While food and clothing provide a momentary life of hope, only the assurance of faith in Christ provides the continual desire to overcome the oppression of poverty. Providing hope for today and tomorrow is the essence of a *whole* gospel.[65]

Spiritual bigotry masquerades as biblical judgment but it is merely blind rejection of whatever we are not comfortable with and a refusal to confront with the reliable measuring rod of essential biblical doctrine.

Throughout this book we have discussed both sides of the problem: destructive, inequitable, and spiritually damaging witch hunting; and constructive, fair, and spiritually edifying biblical discernment. Witch hunting divides the Body of Christ. Biblical discernment protects both doctrinal integrity and scriptural liberty. In the following chapter we will review some unfair accusations that have been made against counter-cult ministries.

HAPTER 9

Counter-Cult Ministries They're Attacking

*T*he answering machine message played back, "Bob and Gretchen, call me as soon as you can. I led somebody really important to the Lord. You'll never believe who it is!" Glenn was a student friend of ours who had worked in cult apologetics for a couple of years. Before we had a chance to return his call, he called back, "So don't you want to know about that really important person who prayed to receive Christ?" He realized that his enthusiasm had gotten away with him when we responded, "Well, as long as it's somebody really important, Glenn. We certainly don't want to get so excited over an ordinary person's conversion." Glenn got our point and went on, "This guy is the son of [one of the most prominent cult leaders in the United States]! It's amazing that he could ever break free. It could only happen by the power of God. And this guy can really help us get the inside scoop on his father's cult."

Imagine Glenn's disappointment when we gently informed him that this same individual had "gotten saved" many times through most of the cult apologetic ministries, crisis centers, and churches in Glenn's region. He had been getting attention with the same unverifiable story for more than a decade. Glenn's frustration showed as he pondered, "Being a cult expert sure does not exempt you from having a fast one pulled on you every once in a while!"

Glenn is right. Christian experts on the cults are not infallible. They can make mistakes, miss some research, or make mistakes in judgment. But most Christians who have been called to cult apologetics develop responsible discernment principles and are generally reliable sources of evangelical response to the world of the cults and the occult. Gentle, constructive advice and expectations of professional integrity are welcomed by cult watchers. Witch hunting attacks are not.

The Spiritual Counterfeits Project, *Cornerstone* magazine (Jesus People USA), and Christian Research Institute have all been targets of witch hunting. All three of these organizations are highly respected across the country as reliable, evangelical, counter-cult organizations.[1] Despite the solid record of good research, evaluation, and judgment practiced by each of these organizations, all three have been attacked, thanks to witch hunting tactics.

SPIRITUAL COUNTERFEITS PROJECT

Spiritual Counterfeits Project has been accused (along with cofounder Brooks Alexander and former director Karen Hoyt) of being a front organization for the New Age Movement, of consorting with New Agers, and of publishing pro-New Age material in the guise of critical evaluation.

The Background

Spiritual Counterfeits Project began during the Jesus Movement of the late 1960s and early 1970s. First it was a part of a larger Christian evangelism group in Berkeley called the Christian World Liberation Front (CWLF). Berkeley Christian Coalition (BCC) spun off from CWLF, and Spiritual Counterfeits Project (SCP) spun off from BCC. SCP is one of the oldest, continually active counter-cult organizations in the United States and was the first to concentrate on exposing the ascendancy of New Age thought in America.

Almost eleven years ago we, Dave Hunt, and many other representatives of counter-cult organizations met in Berkeley for a conference on the cults. In 1979 the new cults were spreading like wildfire throughout the United States. Those of us who previously worked quietly and almost without notice were suddenly in demand by Christians, churches, organizations, periodicals, as well as the secular media to provide answers to the looming threat of cultism in America. Not only were cults enjoying unprecedented popularity, but many of their new converts were young people—teenagers and those in their early twenties who left their parents, friends, and other family members for the false gospels of the cults.

During that conference in 1979 we discussed many different issues relating to the cults, theology, sociology, psychology, and doctrine. We shared information, listened to lectures, dialogued, and sometimes disagreed with each other in Christian love and professional respect.

That conference was sponsored by SCP—then and now noted for its in-depth information about and analysis of Eastern and occultic movements in the United States. SCP had been instrumental in the united Christian court action which effectively removed the teaching of Transcendental Meditation from the New Jersey public schools in 1977. SCP had also done pioneering research and evangelism with the thousands of young people who "turned on" to both drugs and Eastern mysticism in the sixties and seventies.

Today SCP is a highly respected source of in-depth and biblical evaluation of alternate belief systems—especially Eastern and New Age systems.

The Charges

According to Constance Cumbey, SCP could very well be working for the New Age Movement rather than for the gospel of Jesus Christ. This is a serious charge against an organization with a longer track record of accurate biblical discernment than the length of Cumbey's whole ministry. For such a charge to be backed up, there would have to be abundant and univocal proof. There is no such proof, but even protestations of defense by SCP are viewed as being more "evidence" of SCP's duplicity.

Here are some of the reasons Cumbey gives for believing that SCP is actually working for the New Age Movement:[2]

1. David Spangler, a prominent New Ager, allegedly recommended the new SCP book, *The New Age Rage*.
2. David Spangler, other New Agers, evangelicals, Pentecostals, and SCP all attended a by-invitation-only "reconciliation" conference in Colorado in October 1987.
3. *The New Age Rage* lists ten issues SCP has in

common with the New Age Movement, and says there are many more not listed.

4. When Cumbey tried to get copies of the tapes from that conference from SCP, the staff held an emergency meeting and then said no tapes had ever been made.

5. Karen Hoyt, former executive director of SCP, attended that conference.

6. SCP distributed a paper disagreeing with Cumbey.

7. CWLF and BCC (SCP forerunners) have been listed in and referred to by New Age publications.

8. BCC's *Radix* magazine and *Sojourners* had interlocking editors, and both are definitely New Age and extreme left wing.

9. Brooks Alexander, cofounder of SCP, is two-faced. He knew SCP's newsletter had recommended Jeremy Rifkin's New Age book *The Emerging Order*, but he told Cumbey in 1983 that "any evangelical who fell for it proved the end was near," and then in 1985 he pretended he did not know SCP had once endorsed the book.

10. *The New Age Rage* is published by Revell, which has published numerous New Age books.

The Evaluation

When we interviewed Brooks Alexander on these charges, he asked us a question that cuts to the core of one witch hunting technique: "Why always accept at face value the words of heretics, enemies of the gospel, New Agers, and never even ask for or believe responses from those who are supposed to be brothers and sisters in the Lord?"[3]

We asked for SCP's response to Cumbey's accusations and coupled their answers with some logical thinking. The conclusion: SCP is clearly not a New

Age front, but is, as it has been for more than seventeen years, strongly within the center of biblical orthodoxy and compassionate analysis and evangelism of non-Christians.

A witch hunting attitude says, "I'm so sure of the accusation I'm making that any evidence you show me that disagrees with my accusation must just be a sign of your clever cover-up." It's like Roscoe, faced with evidence that Bob could not have been a Jesuit spy responding, "Only a Jesuit would be that clever!"

We call this the "no-elephants-in-Connecticut" attitude. There once was a man who took the daily train from New York to Connecticut every morning and evening. One morning he sat in a different car, next to a man he had never seen. The other man had a box of paper clips on his lap, and every five seconds he threw one out the train window. He never said a word. That evening our commuter went to the same car, hoping the see the paper clip man. There he was, silently throwing paper clips out the window. The commuter started sitting next to this man every day. The man never said a word, he just kept throwing paper clips out the window. Finally, our commuter could stand it no longer. "Why in the world do you always throw paper clips out the window?" The man looked carefully about, debating whether he could be trusted. Finally he whispered, "It scares the elephants away!"

Our commuter suppressed a broad grin as he patiently explained, "But there are no elephants in Connecticut!"

"Exactly," the man nodded vigorously, "see how well it works!"

Like our elephant story, many of the "proofs" used to show the connection between SCP and the New Age Movement are not proofs at all. They do as good a job of convicting SCP of being New Age as paper clips do keeping elephants out of Connecticut. Accusation numbers 1, 3, 4, 6, 7, 8, and 10 fall into this category.

David Spangler is free to recommend or reject any publication he wishes, even *The New Age Rage,* without permission or authority from SCP. Certainly SCP has no legal right to forbid his recommendation. If they have *no* real connection with the New Age Movement, then they certainly would have no influence or power over Spangler to pressure him into withdrawing his recommendation of their book. Whether Spangler recommended the book or not has nothing to do with SCP's involvement with or opposition to the New Age Movement. It would not be the first time a non-Christian endorsed a Christian. Even the apostle Paul received an unsolicited endorsement from a demoniac in Acts 19:16–18! In fact, Cumbey, in the same talk, referred to a New Age bookstore that carried *her* book for a time. Are we to believe she is a plant for the New Age Movement because a New Age bookstore sold her book?

This is the same principle by which we answer her charges listed as numbers 7, 8, and 10. SCP has no power over who will or will not mention them in the public media. Brooks Alexander speculated to us that one reason some New Agers are familiar with SCP is simply that SCP is actively engaged in reaching New Agers for Christ—they care enough to risk their reputation by getting involved personally with nonbelievers, without compromising the gospel, but sharing the truth in love. We might add that in a similar way Jesus risked his reputation by associating with those he was trying to reach. This resulted, due to witch hunting tactics of his day, in his being mislabeled a glutton and a drunkard and a friend of sinners (Matt. 11:19). We should be so honored to receive such criticism for doing God's work! It may be Cumbey's opinion that both SCP and *Sojourners* are "definitely New Age and extreme left wing," but responsible, well-respected evangelical authorities who have done their homework don't agree with her.

We don't agree with *Sojourners* economic theories, for example, but we cannot on that basis condemn them or their editor for heresy. We certainly cannot condemn SCP for having an editor in common with *Sojourners*. Cumbey presented no proof in her talk that the organizations, their publications, or their editors teach New Age heresy. Finally, condemning SCP because its book was published by a company that also publishes New Age books is just as bad as condemning Hal Lindsey's *The Road to Holocaust* because it was published by a publisher that publishes New Age books.[4] It is purely guilt by association. SCP cannot control which books their publisher accepts or rejects. And, in fact, if they designed *The New Age Rage* as an evangelism tool, then it would be more likely to get into the hands of New Agers who need its message if it is published by a publisher of New Age books.

During her talk, Cumbey read from the preface to *The New Age Rage* where Karen Hoyt, executive director of SCP, listed ten issues "where there can be some agreement with NAM."[5] The ten issues summarized are as follows:

1. Cooperation instead of competition (personal, not economic)
2. Protection of the creation (earth's resources)
3. Creativity and spontaneity
4. Promoting peace
5. Radical transformation "even though our idea

of the needed change is very different from
NAM's"[6]
6. Bodily care
7. Human potential and positive self-image—not
unlimited potential, self-marred through sin
8. Global village—"a crisis in one country affects
the whole world"[7]
9. Working for a nontoxic environment
10. Networking—the Christian Church

Are these ten areas of "some agreement" really in-
dicators that SCP is part of the New Age Movement?
If so, then the Bible must be a New Age handbook
after all.

1. Exodus 17:12 gives us an example of godly men
cooperating to help Moses serve the Lord; Philippians 2:12–13 describes the cooperation between
God and man in sanctification; and, most importantly, Psalm 119:63 and Romans 14:1 reveal that
the basis of biblical cooperation is obedience to
God and faith.
2. Genesis 1:26,28 provides the ultimate master
plan for creation: "'Let Us make man in Our image, according to Our likeness; let them have
dominion over . . . all the earth and over every
creeping thing that creeps on the earth'. . . . Then
God blessed them, and God said to them, 'Be fruit-
ful and multiply; fill the earth and subdue it; have
dominion over the fish of the sea, over the birds of
the air, and over every living thing that moves on
the earth.'"
3. Proverbs 31:10–31, in describing the "excellent
wife," gives attributes fitting for both men and
women, and stresses the imaginative, creative,
and industrious attributes which confirm this

ideal person as a fulfilled reflection of the image of God in redeemed mankind.

4. Philippians 4:7 reveals that true peace comes from God; Christ is referred to as the Prince of Peace (Isa. 9:6) and he said, "Blessed are the peacemakers, for they shall be called sons of God" (Matt. 5:9). Peace is established by God (Isa. 26:12), and world peace will be established in the end (Rev. 21, 22). Christians are commanded to live in peace (2 Cor. 13:11) and pursue peace (2 Tim. 2:22).

5. Second Corinthians 5:16–17 describes the radical transformation SCP and Christians identify with the justifying and sanctifying work of the gospel. Paul refers to this transformation in the radical terms of "death" and "life"; "old man" and "new man" (Rom. 6). In Romans 12:1–2 Paul commands all Christians to reject conformation to the world, but to be transformed "by the renewing of your mind."

6. First Corinthians 6:15–20 provides the Christian context for taking care of our bodies. The apostle Paul admonishes, "For you were bought at a price; therefore glorify God in your body and in your spirit, which are God's."

7. Philippians 1:6 affirms the biblical basis for human potential and positive "self-image" *based on the redeeming and sanctifying work of the Holy Spirit:* "Being confident of this very thing, that He who has begun a good work in you will complete it until the day of Jesus Christ." This is echoed in Hebrews 10:39, "But we are not of those who draw back to perdition, but of those who believe to the saving of the soul."

8. Luke 10:30–37 gives us one of the best exam-

ples of a biblical "global village" attitude: the Good Samaritan did not let ethnic diversity, different nationalities, or even the fact that he was on a journey away from his own land get in the way of his obligation before God to be a "neighbor" to anyone in need.

9. Genesis 1:26–28, quoted earlier, gives us the pattern for keeping our world toxin free, and Genesis 2:15 echoes, "Then the Lord God took the man and put him in the garden of Eden to tend and keep it." It is a general biblical principle that we must be good stewards of whatever resources God entrusts us with—the earth (certainly) included.

10. Romans 16:1–16 gives us one of the best examples of the apostle Paul's frequent "networking" among the early churches. He introduces Phoebe to the Roman church; sends greetings to his old friends Priscilla and Aquila and the church in their home; and sends greetings to at least twenty-six friends by name "and all the saints who are with them."

Though Cumbey certainly would not want to accuse the Bible of being New Age, by using the test she applied to SCP, the Bible would certainly qualify. Obviously, her test must be faulty.

Often those who engage in witch hunting see conspiracy in everything, whether there is objective evidence for all conspiracy or not. Cumbey tried to get copies of the secret Boulder New Age conference tapes from SCP based on her belief that SCP had attended and been given tapes. She says that the SCP researcher she talked with called her back to say that, after an emergency staff meeting, she was told that "no tapes had been made." From this conversation, Cumbey assumes that SCP must be covering up their own duplicity in the affair. (See reason number 4).

We checked with SCP for their explanation. They were not invited to the conference. One of their trustees, Art Lindsley, from the C. S. Lewis Institute, was invited, but not as a representative from SCP. SCP was not represented at the conference.[8] (This refutes reasons number 2 and 5.) They had no knowledge of any conference tapes. The "emergency meeting" had nothing to do with Cumbey's call.

Whom do we believe? Cumbey or SCP? Without corroborating evidence, there is no reason to believe Cumbey's surmises. And 1 Tim. 5:19 says, "Do not receive an accusation against an elder except from two or three witnesses." The truthfulness of SCP's official explanation flows naturally from their excellent track record of combating heresy and upholding orthodoxy. Cumbey may think she sees a conspiracy here, but she presented no hard evidence.

The same is true concerning Cumbey's unwarranted assumption that SCP's position paper concerning her was prompted by the perceived threat of her exposing them as New Agers. (See reason number 6.) But she has created a catch-22: if SCP agrees with her, she's right; but if they disagree with her, that *proves* she's right! On the contrary, the SCP position paper was written for the same reason religion scholar, J. Gordon Melton, then later Walter Martin's Christian Research Institute, *Cornerstone* magazine, and we made our positions public. It was in response to unwarranted accusations and suppositions by Cumbey, and in response to literally hundreds of inquiries from the public.

Anyone who examines Cumbey's charge against Brooks Alexander (see reason number 9) can see that it is meritless. First, recommendation of Jerry

Rifkin's *The Emerging Order* does not necessarily mean that SCP is New Age. The context or limitation with which a publication is recommended is crucial. For example, we recommend reading *The Humanist Manifesto I* and *II* for anyone who thinks secular humanism is a benign personal inclination by a few harmless individuals. The shock value is worth the recommendation. Anti-abortionist Bernard Nathanson recommends viewing *The Silent Scream* and *The Eclipse of Reason,* each film containing footage of actual abortions. He recommends it for anyone who thinks abortion is a simple medical procedure done to excise a blob of tissue. Does he approve of the abortions shown in those films? Of course not! Viewing the carnage firsthand is more persuasive against abortion than argumentation alone. In the same way, recommending Rifkin's book is not necessarily the same as agreeing with the book.

Second, Cumbey wrongly accused Brooks of pretending he did not know SCP had once endorsed the book. According to her,[9] she talked with Brooks on the phone and hinted about an unnamed organization that actively promoted Rifkin's book. She says she deliberately led him on and deceived him before she revealed that SCP was the target of her "Twenty Questions" game. Is she good at duplicity? If she is, then Brooks cannot be faulted for falling for it.

Summary

This analysis of accusations against SCP exposes the very worst in witch hunting. Through the use of innuendo, bad thinking, and lapses in logic, a Christian organization which has proven its dedication to the gospel and its faithfulness to essential biblical doctrine has been maligned. It is impossible to square this with Christian ethics. Scripture says, "Do not accuse a man for no reason—when he has done you no harm" (Prov. 3:30 NIV).

CORNERSTONE MAGAZINE

Cornerstone magazine and its parent organization (Jesus People USA) have suffered from attack on its assistant editor, Eric Pement, who has been accused of compromising with New Age beliefs, lying about his conversation with Constance Cumbey, and of passing himself off as an expert on the New Age Movement without adequate research. The magazine and organization have also been accused of fostering one-word socialist ideas because they live in Christian community and share their possessions.

The Background

Eric Pement is an assistant editor of *Cornerstone* magazine, published by Jesus People USA (JPUSA) in Chicago. JPUSA is one of the oldest successful evangelical Christian communities, with roots in the Jesus Movement of the late 1960s. In addition to publishing, the more than one hundred families in JPUSA run a ministry. They serve the hungry, poor, and needy of their Chicago neighborhood; evangelize through the messages of their world-famous Christian rock band, "Rez" (formerly, "Resurrection Band"); provide rehabilitation and housing for alcohol- and drug-dependent individuals; provide discipleship and job training for new converts; and coordinate many different evangelism outreaches. They also sponsor an annual summer music festival and Christian training event that draws thousands of registrants from all over the country.

Eric Pement is *Cornerstone*'s expert on the cults. He has been a competent researcher and writer in the field for years and regularly contributes to other periodicals, as well as to *Cornerstone*. Pement is on the Board of Directors of the Evangelical Ministries to New Religions (EMNR), the cult apologetics organization coalition chaired by Dr. Gordon Lewis of Denver Seminary in Colorado.

The Charges

Constance Cumbey has accused Pement of many failings, including deliberate lying.

It is very serious for Cumbey to charge Pement with deliberate lying. God calls lying an abomination (Prov. 6:16–19). The liar is promised judgment by God (Prov. 19:5), and Revelation 21:8,27 promises that those whose lives are characterized by lies will spend eternity in the lake of fire! Cumbey said in her interview that Pement kept telling people he had talked with her extensively on the telephone when actually he had only talked with her for "all of ten minutes." She went on, "He's an absolute liar!"

In addition to calling Pement a liar, Cumbey proceeded on this radio program to tear at Pement's professional credibility. She claimed he "did absolutely no research," was unfamiliar with Unification theology, "had done no homework on the New Age Movement," had admitted to her that he had not read one word of Alice Bailey,[10] and was into communal living—"one of the pushes of the New Age Movement."[11] For someone who has been researching, writing, and reporting on cultic and occultic phenomena for years (he joined JPUSA in 1976, years before Cumbey began her research), and whose magazine has published since its inception

216

articles critical of beliefs and practices now labeled
New Age, such charges seem incredible. It's interesting to note that Cumbey made these sweeping
dismissals of a recognized writer and ministry on
the basis of what she claims was a telephone call of
"all of ten minutes long."

The Evaluation

We have a transcript of this infamous phone call,
which actually lasted over one hour. Pement demonstrated excellent knowledge of New Age thought,
although, in keeping with his primary role as inter-
viewer, he attempted to concentrate on asking questions rather than discussing his own research and
conclusions. He researched New Age thought and
practices for years prior to his conversation with
Cumbey and has kept up with his research since
that time.

Cumbey accused Pement of not knowing Unification theology because he questioned her statement
that the Moonies were part of the great conspiracy of
the New Age Movement. Pement questioned
Cumbey's assumption on the basis that Moon was
hardly likely to support the installation of the New
Age Maitreya as the New Age Christ since he believes himself to be the Lord of the Second Advent!

Pement never said that he had not read one word
of Alice Bailey. The transcript reveals that he said he
had not yet read Bailey's *Externalization of the Hierarchy*. There are literally hundreds of New Age writers and thousands of New Age books, and although
Bailey is significant, one does not have to have read
all of her books to be knowledgeable of New Ageism.
Pement was very well read in New Age material and,
in fact, had read other Bailey writings.

Finally, to attack JPUSA for being "into communal living," which she identifies as one of the pushes of the New Age Movement, is simply name-calling. It is true that most of the hippie communes were characterized by sexual "freedom" and copious drug use. But communal living, by definition, merely means living in community, close together and under one organization.

JPUSA's families choose to pool their resources and share their assets as a freewill response of their commitment to Jesus Christ and their loving Christian commitment to each other. There is no immorality, drug or alcohol abuse, and there is solid doctrinal Christian trustworthiness. Indictment of JPUSA because they are "into communal living" can only be sustained if Cumbey wants also to indict a small group of New Testament Christians who were similarly "into communal living":

> Now all who believed were together, and had all things in common, and sold their possessions and goods, and divided them among all, as anyone had need. So continuing daily with one accord in the temple, and breaking bread from house to house, they ate their food with gladness and simplicity of heart, praising God and having favor with all the people. And the Lord added to the church daily those who were being saved (Acts 2:44–47).

Summary

Pement is very slow to anger, doesn't hold grudges, and probably has fewer "enemies" than almost anyone else in cult apologetics. Speaking of Cumbey's attacks, not only against him, he said,

> I suppose, to me, the Connie Cumbey rift signifies something I wish never would have happened. We for-

got to disagree in love and in respect for the other person. I really feel sorry that we couldn't have re-called our identities as committed Christians, first and foremost, so as to offset whatever differences we had in terms of analysis of the New Age Movement. . . . When Connie and I met at that catastrophic meeting back in March [1983]—with Jim Valentine, Jim Sire, Dawn [Herrin], Jon Trott, and later Rabi [Maharaj]—I suppose one of the reasons it was such a shattering experience for me was that Jesus was left completely out of the picture. When Connie and all of us sat down at the table, the air was so tense it was difficult to say "we were gathered in His name."

I suppose Constance thought we were going to have her for breakfast, so the alternative was to eat us up first. We didn't come there to prove ourselves right, to shame her with our expertise, or to play Old Boy Club, Getting the New Kid in Town. We came to share, to learn, to seek an explanation, to set forth some of our views, and to ask that we might reason together. It's true that I thought she's in error in some points (I've detailed these in my article and in the preceding pages), but I'd hoped we could rationally discuss them and come to mutual agreement or at least closer together. Instead I was castigated as inept, a dummy, and a liar. I really couldn't have been more shocked or hurt at the way things turned out.

. . . . The fact remains that it has been a real stumbling block to people she feels are "against" her or who disagree with her views. A lot of people have had a pretty rough treatment at her hands, both publicly and privately. This isn't the dog-eat-dog, kill-or-be-killed business world, this is among Christians, co-laborers, and fellow workers in reaching the lost in the cults, the occult, and the empty religious philosophies of today. I know that a lot of people have re-

219

ceived far worse treatment than they merited, and I'm not referring to my own experience by any means. If Connie expects to flourish and grow as a believer, she will have to do it within the Christian community, not outside of it, but in a church or assembly where she can grow and experience the give-and-take, the nurture, as well as the reproof, of Christian ministers and pastors.[12]

CHRISTIAN RESEARCH INSTITUTE AND WALTER MARTIN

Before his death in June 1989, Walter Martin had been at the forefront of cult apologetics for more than thirty-five years. His Christian Research Institute, founded in 1960, has done more to protect people from the cults and evangelize cultists than any other counter-cult ministry. When he began writing and speaking on the cults in the early 1950s, he met opposition from almost every quarter. American churches seemed unmotivated to meet and beat the challenge of the cults, and the secular world viewed cult apologetics as narrow-minded, fundamentalist nit-picking. The cults, of course, claimed he was discriminating against them, unfairly attacking them, and holding them up to ridicule. But Martin, through his lectures, radio program ("The Bible Answer Man" was heard daily across the country), books, and cassette tapes, provided a consistent, biblically based defense of the Christian faith against the myriad of claims by the cults. His classic textbook, *The Kingdom of the Cults,* has appeared frequently on Christian best-seller lists since its first edition appeared in 1965. Today *The Kingdom of the Cults* has proved itself the standard evangelical work on the major American cults.

The Christian Research Institute (CRI) was founded by Martin as a unique ministry of research, publication, and library resources concentrated on cult apologetics. Through the staff of CRI, thousands of Christians throughout the world have received sound biblical responses to the claims of the cults, and thousands of cultists have been exposed to the truth of the biblical gospel. *The Christian Research Journal* has developed from a small newsletter in the 1970s to the premier professional journal of Christian counter-cult apologetics.

The Charges

Christian Research Institute (CRI) has suffered criticism throughout its existence, typically from two different directions: Christians, who fail to understand the threat of cultic gospels, accuse CRI of being judgmental; and non-Christians, mostly cultists, accuse CRI of defending its own partisan interpretation of the Bible against *their* interpretation.

Rarely, however, has CRI been criticized for not properly representing the beliefs and scope of the cults. During the last few years, though, Constance Cumbey has decided that since CRI and Martin disagree with her analysis in certain areas, they must be sinfully wrong—perhaps even to the point of secret collusion with the New Age Movement!

In *A Planned Deception* Cumbey quoted Martin, saying,

> "The New Age movement got its start in 1978 and took its name from the name of a magazine," Dr. Walter Martin, "Bible Answer Man" program, Fall, 1983. . . .

Despite Dr. Martin's ill-advised statement, the New Age movement certainly did not begin "yesterday."[13]

In the same book she also charged,

Not all Christian cult authorities have agreed with my analysis. Dr. Walter Martin has said, "Don't worry about it. It's only occultism." My reply is that occultism is what the Bible warned us of as the eternal Mystery Babylon which had corrupted all nations. It is not "mere occultism" or "mere idolatry." This is what since time immemorial has brought God's wrath down upon its practitioners and a society professing God, but continuing to tolerate it. And God's wrath was not so poured out upon the idolatrous heathen as it was his corrupt body who should have known better. No doubt, Isaiah, Jeremiah, Ezekiel, Amos and the other prophets were faced with the specter of false prophets of their day saying, "It's only occultism, go back to sleep—you're wrong, it's not in the church!"[14]

During a radio program on Portland, Oregon station KPDQ Cumbey said,

Walter Martin and a number of others got together and organized a conference in Denver in 1985. I was the only person in the country who was not invited. They hired security guards to keep me away.[15]

The aggregate of Cumbey's repeated references to the late Walter Martin, CRI, and Elliot Miller (CRI senior literary consultant) are that they are—perhaps deliberately—suppressing information about and responses to the New Age Movement. In some way, shape, or form, they operate more as agents of the New Age Movement than as cult apologists.

The Evaluation

We already discussed part of the problem between Cumbey and CRI. As our earlier citation from *Christianity Today* stated, Cumbey tends to come across as someone who assumes anyone who disagrees with her must be an agent of the enemy. This is one of the most common witch hunting habits and one that any of us can slip into when we forget to look at all sides of an issue and explore all of the alternatives.

When Cumbey first began criticizing CRI and Martin several years before Martin's death, we talked with him and asked for his response. He first explained that he had no problem with people disagreeing with him. He had faced that throughout his ministry. But he felt Cumbey's criticisms were unfair: First, because they misrepresented his position; second, because they unnecessarily divided the Body of Christ; third, because they took time and resources to answer that should have been spent on defending the gospel; and fourth, because they confused lay people, who might ignore the threats of the New Age Movement because they didn't understand why the professionals were fighting about it so much. Here is the statement he gave us then:

> My research work in the fields of the cults and the occult have been reviewed by the best evangelical scholarship in contemporary Christendom. I am content to rest with their evaluation. . . . Apparently Mrs. Cumbey believes that anyone who disagrees with her findings is suspect as either a friend or member of the New Age Conspiracy. This smacks of religious McCarthyism and has no place in Christian ethics. . . .
>
> I think Constance Cumbey has spent a great deal of time going over old ground that has been successfully

dealt with by others. She has also fostered a type of religious paranoia concerning the alleged monolithic threat of the New Age Movement. I would recommend to her some extensive study in Christian theology, apologetics, and church history, about which she appears to have limited knowledge, as her writings reflect. The study of law is no substitute for these disciplines.[16]

Cumbey's vehement and repeated charges against CRI had to be answered, both to affirm CRI's credibility in cult apologetics and to provide balanced, biblical help to those who are victims of the New Age Movement. CRI's Senior Literary Consultant, Elliot Miller, prepared an eleven-page response paper to Cumbey's major charges, and we will quote extensively from it here.[17]

Cumbey misquoted Martin concerning the origin of the New Age Movement. Here is exactly what he said, transcribed from a tape of the broadcast in question, along with Miller's commentary:

> This supposed quote from Dr. Martin, which Mrs. Cumbey has repeated over and over again as the most condemning evidence against him, provides a good example of why we have been critical of her methodology. She has not only taken Dr. Martin out of context, she has misquoted him. The actual statement, made on "The Bible Answer Man" program of December 3, 1983, was as follows:
>
>> The word "New Age movement," incidentally, is the title of a magazine. That's where the phrase was coined. It wasn't coined by Constance Cumbey. It was coined in a magazine entitled the *New Age*. And I think it was as far back as the mid-1970s that we were getting this.

The reader should note the following points: first, Walter Martin never said that the New Age movement (NAM) "got its start in 1978," nor did he imply that it began "yesterday". . . .

Second, in spite of Mrs. Cumbey's repeated affirmations to the contrary, neither here nor anywhere else has Dr. Martin denied that the NAM has historical roots in Theosophy. . . .

And, while Dr. Martin's suggestion that the phrase was "coined" by the *New Age Journal* could fairly be disputed, it can certainly be argued that that influential magazine's name strongly contributed to the popularization and final acceptance of the term "New Age" as the movement's name.[18]

This is CRI's response to the charge that Martin wanted people to "go back to sleep," to ignore the New Age Movement:

No documentation is given for a quote which seems out of character with Walter Martin.

Although it is doubtful that Dr. Martin said those exact words . . . it is likely that *something* was said, which Mrs. Cumbey misheard and misunderstood. It is likely that the original statement was made to calm the hysteria that Cumbey was creating with her claim that, in all probability, the Antichrist would appear in a matter of weeks or months.

Dr. Martin offered this reply:

If I made the statement, it was in this context: The New Age Movement is not some new phenomenon never encountered or fought by the church. It is "only" occultism dressed up in new vocabulary and style. Don't worry that the church can't answer it or prevail against it: we've been combatting the same ideas and spiritual powers since the Fall. It is ridiculous for Mrs. Cumbey to ascribe complacency to me when I have dedicated my life (over many more years than Mrs. Cumbey) to waking people up to such dangers, and to preaching salvation to those who are lost. . . .[19]

In the months since Dr. Martin's death, we have seen and heard hundreds of individuals and almost every cult apologetics organization in the country credit Dr. Martin and the ministry of CRI with being the inspiration for their own efforts to combat false belief. To tie the "father" of American cult apologetics to a New Age suppression conspiracy is absurd.

We also carefully investigated Cumbey's charges that she was, in effect, barred from the 1985 Denver cults conference, that security guards were hired to keep her out, and that Walter Martin spearheaded this organized suppression. We talked independently with several of the people who organized the conference and with several people who attended. No one with direct knowledge backed up Cumbey's claims. Dr. Gordon Lewis of Denver Seminary, host of the conference, confirmed that Cumbey was not asked to be a speaker or to make a presentation at the conference, but that she was welcome to attend just like anyone else. There were many professional cult apologists who attended without being speakers. They didn't feel discriminated against. It was not a closed meeting, and those who attended without receiving personal invitations didn't feel slighted either. Miller notes,

Dr. Martin was a speaker there, but . . . he was not involved in the conference's planning and organization. . . . It's true that Mrs. Cumbey was not invited to speak (which is no more strange than Walter Martin's not being invited to speak at certain end-time prophecy conferences where Cumbey is a featured attraction). However, she was more than welcome to attend. The claim that there were security guards hired to keep her out is both false (this writer was there) and preposterous.[20]

Summary

CRI's defense closes with a summary that highlights some of the most damaging consequences of witch hunting, no matter who inadvertently slips into inappropriate judgment:

Mrs. Cumbey's heated and bitter denunciations of Walter Martin and CRI in public forums has surely been detrimental to the cause of Christ. The casual listener (Christian or non-Christian) would tend to be appalled at such animosity coming out of the mouth of a representative of Christ. And it's not even directed at the enemies of the gospel, but at someone involved in the same kind of Christian work! Ultimately, it is the credibility of Constance Cumbey that suffers most.[21]

AVOIDING WITCH HUNTING

Walter Martin was a personal friend as well as a colleague, and over the eighteen years we knew him, he gave us many wise insights into apologetics. Three of the principles he taught us have played an important part in helping us avoid witch hunting in our own ministry.

We learned the first principle shortly after we met

Dr. Martin in 1972. We were standing with him at the back of an auditorium where he had just given a talk on Jehovah's Witnesses. Two young women came up. The older one introduced herself as a Christian and her sister as a Jehovah's Witness who wanted to know the truth. Although Dr. Martin was tired, his eyes lit up and he seemed to be infused with energy as he began to speak. He gently and carefully shared the gospel with the young Jehovah's Witness, Jan, and then patiently answered all of the Watchtower objections she raised. After the first hour, she seemed to be stuck on the Jehovah's Witness translation of John 1:1, which makes the Word (Jesus) "a god." Dr. Martin explained the English, the theology, the exegesis, the New Testament Greek—nothing seemed to get through to Jan. Frustrated, she blurted out, "But how do you *know* what the right translation is?" Dr. Martin paused for a moment, and we eagerly anticipated an intellectually and academically erudite response. Then Dr. Martin spoke, "Jan, I know what I know. I know what the truth is. And the truth is in Jesus Christ, not the Watchtower." Dr. Martin taught us always to put Christ first.

Another time we were sitting in Dr. Martin's living room and he was telling us stories about how, as a young Bible college student, he had battled the atheists who used to "street preach" in New York City. After four or five good stories we asked, "How do you learn the principles for answering so many hundreds of kinds of objections to faith?" Dr. Martin answered, "There are many ways to learn, and I do a little of each one. But what helps me learn principles and how to explain them to someone else is that I always learn from others. You never get too smart or too knowledgeable to learn from others. Lots of times people think they're getting answers from me, but I'm picking their brains at the same time!" Dr. Martin's commitment was proof that there is wisdom and safety in a multitude of counselors.

When it came to persuasive speaking, nobody was better than Walter Martin. He held every one of his audiences in the palm of his hand. He knew the stories to tell, the emotion behind his words, the pictures to draw with words so that people would understand his message and be motivated to do something about it. We commented offhandedly one time to him that it was probably easier for him to persuade an audience than for most of the rest of us to, because he was such a dynamic communicator. "Hold on," he interjected, "it's harder for me than it is for you." And he explained that a gift of communication is a curse as well as a blessing, "Before I became a Christian and God called me to the ministry, I had planned to be a trial attorney. Even as a youngster I understood the power of words, and I was pretty good even then at convincing people to believe me. But when I became a Christian I knew that persuasiveness was a lie if it wasn't used to promote the truth which is in Christ. I've always had to guard against the temptation to let my vigil for the truth slip because it's so easy to do it the other way." Dr. Martin was committed to the truth, even when it was so much easier to promote what was persuasive but wrong.

The Christian who adopts these three principles will protect himself from witch hunting and will have the proper weapons for judging between the truth and a lie.

THE SAD RESULTS OF WITCH HUNTING

There is no excuse for Christians to engage in witch hunting, even in an effort to promote good (Rom. 3:7–8). In Titus 3 Paul admonishes Christians "to speak evil of no one, to be peaceable, gentle, showing all humility to all men" (v. 2), and warns that false accusations characterize nonbelievers rather than Christians:

> Reject a divisive man after the first and second admonition, knowing that such a person is warped and sinning, being self-condemned (vv. 10–11).

As Christians we are commanded to test all things and to discern truth from error. But when our tests are inadequate, when we sacrifice truth for expediency, and when we end up snaring the innocent and unwittingly exonerating the guilty, then our discernment degenerates into witch hunting.

Witch hunting hurts its targets, those who compromise their standards by practicing it and those who are searching for biblical truth.

CHAPTER 10

Learning Responsible Discernment

*T*he real battle is between the Church and the world, not within the Church. The refrain of orthodoxy goes, "In necessary things, unity; in doubtful things, liberty; in all things, charity."

When we practice the admonition "in necessary things, unity," we learn right doctrine, which results in right worship and right action. We also distinguish ourselves clearly from the world and from competing religious systems.

When we practice "in doubtful things, liberty," we promote biblical unity in the Body of Christ; we strengthen each other, we bring each other into maturity as Christians, and we allow for the diversity that provides new believers with fellowships specially molded to their specific needs. We also proclaim our Christian transformation to the world by our well-rounded, orderly diversity in unity.

When we practice "in all things, charity," we distinguish between the immature and the heretical; the ignorant and the deceivers; the fallible and the egoists. We demonstrate our Christian commitment by our love.

AVOIDING WITCH HUNTING

We have surveyed some of the most common problems that occur when we attempt to practice biblical judgment without biblical preparation. The threat of these problems should not make us afraid to challenge hostile beliefs and systems we face daily both within the Church and in the world. On the contrary, the Bible commands us to defend the faith (Jude 3), but reasonably and gently (1 Pet. 3:15), and with the full armor of God (Eph. 6:10ff).

We have not only surveyed problems, we have also reviewed the essentials of Christian faith and the importance of both preserving unity and pointing out heresy. Finally, we have examined biblical principles that can be trusted to help us distinguish truth from heresy.

CHARACTERISTICS OF WITCH HUNTING

Witch hunting is a misguided attempt to protect oneself from heresy without using biblical means to do so. We do not have to depend on slipshod, unpredictable, illogical, and unbiblical techniques to protect us from the Enemy. Check the list below. Do you know someone with some of these characteristics who has been "witch hunted"? Have you, perhaps unwittingly, used one or more of these techniques in an unsuccessful attempt to protect yourself from the cults? Determine now to trade characteristics of witch hunting for characteristics of biblical discernment.

1. Lack of association with others in the same field
2. Lack of understanding of theology and church history
3. Lack of a comprehensive worldview
4. Obsession with eschatology
5. Error of guilt by association
6. Error of faulty definitions
7. Error of appeal to inappropriate authority
8. Error of guilt by vocabulary or quote
9. Error of self-refutation and contradiction
10. Error of assuming *similar* means "same"
11. Error of ignoring other possible options
12. Error of using false analogies
13. Ignorance of the value of general revelation

BIBLICAL DISCERNMENT

When we cast aside the errors of witch hunting, we can commit ourselves to biblical discernment. Then we need never fear heresy, and we can be assured that our faithfulness to biblical truth remains intact.

1. Study God's Word. Nothing can substitute for the food of Scripture.

We once knew a young man who was proud of the way he had learned how to witness to Jehovah's Witnesses. "I don't have to spend hour after hour studying doctrine anymore," he said. "I just prove they've made false prophecies and knock 'em flat!" This young man, despite his zeal, was cutting himself off from the necessary biblical foundation, without which he could not maintain his own faith nor offer anything of value to the Jehovah's Witness. Second Timothy 2:15 admonishes, "Be diligent to present

233

yourself approved to God, a worker who does not need to be ashamed, rightly dividing the word of truth." Philippians 2:16 calls it the word of life, and Hebrews 4:12 promises us that it is living and active.

2. Fellowship with other believers. The Church is provided by God as a source of edification, instruction, exhortation, comfort, and fellowship (1 Cor. 7:13–14).

We joined a family-oriented church because we needed the support, encouragement, and prayers of God's people (Heb. 10:25). There's a church near us whose pastor once said that part of the reason so many people felt "comfortable" coming to his church was that no one checked up on members if they missed a few weeks. There was no pressure, he noted. Now we certainly don't advocate gestapo elderships. But at our church, we love each other and know each other well enough that we are concerned when our friends are absent, and we feel blessed when our friends care enough to call us when we're missing, to see if they can pray for us, help us, or encourage us. Regardless of the size of the church we join, it is essential that we become part of a small fellowship in which we hold each other mutually accountable for living and teaching biblical Christianity (1 Tim. 4:16).

3. Learn from our elders. Proverbs 16:31 notes the importance of the elder teaching the younger, and Hebrews 11 reminds us of the spiritual wisdom we can learn from a our "ancestors" in the faith. Paul told Timothy not to let anyone despise him for his youth, but he also declared that spiritual leaders should "first be proved, then let them serve . . . being found blameless" (1 Tim. 3:10). There is also spiritual application in the adage, "It's amazing how smart your parents become between the time you're a teenager and when you grow up."

4. Learn to think straight. The apostle Paul's vocabulary is peppered with phrases like "it seemed reasonable," "I am convinced," and "this is the truth." The apostle Peter pointed out the reasonableness of Christianity, saying, "For we did not follow cunningly devised fables when we made known to you the power and coming of our Lord Jesus Christ, but were eyewitnesses of His majesty" (2 Pet. 1:16).

Someone we know was once confronted with evidence that clearly defeated the argument he was using to refute Jehovah's Witnesses. His response went against every principle of Christian integrity: "That's all right," he replied. "No Witness I've ever used it on has known the difference. It works with them, so why not use it?" Christian ethics, unlike utilitariansim, requires godly means as well as godly ends. And, in the long run, people are won most effectively by arguments that can withstand any test.

Bob was invited to give a lecture at a local atheist club. They wanted him to talk on "The Justification for Religious Belief." He modified it to include the atheists, "The Justification for Any Belief," and then proceeded to argue that atheism is self-contradictory and unreasonable and that, in fact, belief in God is the only way to provide a necessary foundation for the legitimacy of logic and reason. By telling the truth, grappling with the world's ideas, and maintaining Christian standards of straight thinking, Bob was available to be used by the Lord.

5. Preach the gospel. First Corinthians 15:1–4 details for us the scriptural gospel as the death, burial, and resurrection of Jesus Christ for our salvation. This gospel should be at the forefront of our evangelism and apologetics. The apostle Paul, presenting his case before the Greek philosophers on Mars Hill, started with the Resurrection (Acts 17:18) and then backtracked to give the logic behind his gospel when the philosophers didn't understand him (vv. 22–30). Then he ended his discourse by proclaming the gospel of the Resurrection again (v. 31).

One night we went to a Christian's house as "backup," in case he had problems witnessing to the Jehovah's Witnesses he had invited over. He didn't let us speak the entire evening, but spent his time proving to the Witnesses that they were wrong about the end times: Jesus was going to rapture the church before the Great Tribulation, and Israel's becoming a state in 1948 was a signal that the end was near. He talked circles around the Witnesses' puny eschatological knowledge, and they left convinced that he was right about the end times.

But we learned a lesson that night. Because we allowed the night to center on a nonessential, those Witnesses left without hearing about Christ and the power of his resurrection (Phil. 3:10).

6. *Put our faith into action.* A lamp under a basket sheds no light. Salt that remains in the shaker seasons nothing. A Christian who hides in church, or only among Christian friends, is sterile.

We were in a television studio one time, preparing to be interviewed on how to handle problem questions when you witness to nonbelievers. We were talking with the producer, who wanted to know some of the problems we were going to discuss. Then he said, "I don't have any problem dealing with nonbelievers!" Skeptical, we asked him why. "Easy," he replied. "I'm active in my church, I have a Christian job at a Christian television station, and I'm a member of a Christian bicycling club. I don't know any non-Christians to give me problems!"

Do we really believe we serve the God of truth? Do we really believe the gospel of Jesus Christ has the answers for the world in every area of life? Then we should be willing to sacrifice everything to bring that gospel to the world, secure in the knowledge that we will prevail, not by our might or our power, but by the Spirit of the Lord (Zech. 4:6).

BLUEBIRDS AND GRACKLES

Witch hunting doesn't protect the Church. It is destructive. One time years ago, we approached Dr. Martin with a problem. We were impatient with him because he was hesitant about calling the teachings of a particular group cultic. We had invested hundreds of hours in research on this group, and we knew that many of its teachings were unbiblical. We asked Dr. Martin why he was waiting before he publicly criticized them. He didn't answer us directly, he told us a story instead.

One day my teacher and mentor, Dr. Donald Grey Barnhouse, and I were walking in the woods near his home. We were talking about cult apologetics and the need to use accurate biblical judgment in exposing the cults. Dr. Barnhouse, as was his habit, carried his old shotgun with him. His property had persistent problems with grackles, relatives of both the blackbirds and the meadowlarks, who were pests and harmed his garden and killed his beloved bluebird's babies. With his shotgun, Dr. Barnhouse was ready to get a grackle at a moment's notice.

Across the path we saw the leaves rustle. We heard the raucous "caw" of the hated grackle. Still quick de-

237

spite his advanced years, Dr. Barnhouse raised the shotgun and fired. A bird plopped to the ground, motionless. Dr. Barnhouse got to it first, and as I approached he turned. There were tears running down his cheeks. In his hands he held the lifeless bluebird.

Notes

Nobody Likes a Heretic

1. Letter from Georgie Kinyon to Cal Beisner, 5 October 1987.

2. Letter from Eric Pement to Dave Hunt, 11 October 1983.

Chapter 1 Tragedies of the Hunt

1. Norman Geisler, *Ethics: Alternatives and Issues* (Grand Rapids: Zondervan, 1971), 218–219.

2. Harold O. J. Brown, *Heresies* (Garden City, N.Y.: Doubleday, 1984), 447.

3. See, for example, Philip J. Klass, *UFOs Explained* (New York: Random House, 1974).

Chapter 2 Who Is Really Christian?

1. J. Gresham Machen, *The Virgin Birth of Christ* (Grand Rapids: Baker, 1930), 392.

2. Unfortunately, some Christians of our day have softened their stance on this crucial doctrine. This undermines the whole foundation of all Christian belief. It usurps the authority which resides in God's Word and throws it to the whims of human opinion. And though in many cases those who do so continue to hold to other essentials, their students tend to move progressively further from those essentials. (See Harold Lindsell's *Battle for the Bible* for more in-depth explanation and documentation.) So it appears that the message of Isaiah 7:9 has application here: "If you do not stand firm in your faith, you will not stand at all" (NIV).

3. For further information we suggest R. A. Torrey, *What the Bible Teaches* (New York: Revell, 1933); Gerald Bray, *Creeds, Councils and Christ* (Downers Grove: InterVarsity, 1984); and Merrill C. Tenney, *The Bible: The Living Word of Revelation* (Grand Rapids: Zondervan, 1968). Other books are listed in "For Further Reading."

4. See especially Chapters 4 and 5 for examples of these problems.

5. Gerald Bray, *Creeds, Councils and Christ* (Downers Grove: InterVarsity, 1984), 204–207.

6. Ibid.

7. See Louis Berkhof, *The History of Christian Doctrines* (Grand Rapids: Baker, 1937), 264.

8. Bray, 9–10.

9. Philip Schaff, *The Creeds of Christendom, Vol. 1* (Grand Rapids: Baker, 1877, 1919), 5.

Chapter 3 Errors that Create Witch Hunters

1. Anthony M. Coniaris, *Introducing the Orthodox Church* (Minneapolis: Light and Life Publishing Company, 1982), 171.

2. For further information on church history and diversity, see Herbert Bouman, *A Look at Today's Churches—A Comparative Guide* (St. Louis: Concordia, 1980) and Noll, Hatch, Marsden, Wells, and Woodbridge, eds., *Eerdman's Handbook to Christianity in America* (Grand Rapids: Eerdmans, 1983).

3. Texe Marrs, *Dark Secrets of the New Age* (Wheaton: Crossway Books, 1987). Although we use real examples from personal experience, published sources, and others' experiences, our purpose is not to single out individuals. It is, rather, to illustrate witch hunting techniques, which are wrong no matter who uses them, ourselves included. We are not trying to blacklist anyone who is cited in this book.

4. Ibid., 220.

5. See Noll, Hatch, Marsden, Wells, and Woodbridge, eds., *Eerdman's Handbook to Christianity in America* (Grand Rapids: Eerdmans, 1983), 462–485; and the *Los Angeles Times*, "Presbyterians Reject Theologian," 28 February 1987, II:16.

6. J. Barton Payne, *Encyclopedia of Biblical Prophecy* (New York: Harper and Row, 1973), 13.

7. Ibid., 97.

8. Dave Hunt, *Beyond Seduction* (Eugene: Harvest House, 1987).

9. Ibid., 250.

10. *Christianity Today*, 3 September 1983, 56.

11. Constance Cumbey letter to Elliot Miller, 6 June 1982.

12. The conservative, evangelical stances and thorough research of both Elliot Miller and SCP can be tested in their respective books, *A Crash Course on the New Age Movement* (Grand Rapids: Baker, 1989) and *The New Age Rage* (Old Tappan, N.J.: Revell, 1987). Although both books were published after Cumbey's criticisms of them, their quality of research and analysis has been consistent through the years and publicly accessible in various publications and speeches. The books accurately represent their positions during the time Cumbey criticized them.

13. Constance Cumbey, *A Planned Deception* (East Detroit: Pointe Publishers, Inc., 1985), 23.

14. Karen Hoyt and the Spiritual Counterfeits Project, *The New Age Rage* (Old Tappan, N.J.: Revell, 1987), 195.

15. Cumbey, *A Planned Deception*, 53.

16. Jerald and Sandra Tanner, *The Lucifer-God Doctrine* (Salt Lake City: Utah Lighthouse Ministry, 1987).

17. Ibid., 25.

18. Dr. Melton's primary research is exhaustive although his analysis is not from a strictly conservative, evangelical viewpoint.

19. J. Gordon Melton, *The Hidden Dangers of the Rainbow: A Christian Response* (Santa Barbara: The Institute for the Study of American Religion, 1985), 2.

Chapter 4 Fallible "Facts"

1. Personal communication, November 1988.

2. Dave Hunt and T. H. McMahon, *The Seduction of Christianity* (Eugene: Harvest House, 1985), 12.

3. Dave Hunt, "Letters" column, *Cornerstone* 15, 79:15; in response to "Mr. Hunt Needs a Logic Lesson," in *Cornerstone* 15, 78.

4. Ibid., 34.

5. Dennis Fulton, "The Abomination of Psychology," *Believers Fellowship Proclaimer* (Box 4604, Whittier, Calif.: Believers Fellowship, n.d.), 5.

6. Hunt and McMahon, *Seduction*,

7. *Psycho-Heresy* (Santa Barbara: Eastgate Publishers, 1987).

8. Hunt and McMahon, *Seduction*, 205.

9. *Psycho-Heresy*, 18.

10. See "For Further Reading" for books dealing directly with the controversy over psychology.

11. Richard Feynman, *Surely You're Joking, Mr. Feynman* (New York: W. W. Norton and Company, 1985), 70.

12. *The Los Angeles Times,* undated clip, 1985.

13. *The Los Angeles Times,* 16 February 1988.

14. Hunt and McMahon, *Seduction,* 18.

15. *Cornerstone,* 15, 79:34.

16. Dave Hunt, *Beyond Seduction* (Eugene: Harvest House, 1987).

17. Dave Hunt, *Whatever Happened to Heaven?* (Eugene: Harvest House, 1988).

18. C. S. Lewis, *Mere Christianity* (New York: Macmillan, 1974), 174–175.

19. For further information see James R. Moore, "Computer Analysis and the Pauline Corpus," *Christianity for the Tough-Minded,* John Warwick Montgomery, ed. (Minneapolis: Bethany Book House, 1973), 280–288.

20. Constance Cumbey, *Hidden Dangers of the Rainbow* (Shreveport: Huntington House Publishers, 1983).

21. Ibid., 152–153.

Chapter 5 Reason Abuse

1. *Propaganda* (Ann Arbor: WFF 'n Proof Company, 1975), game cover.

2. J. P. Moreland, *Scaling the Secular City* (Grand Rapids: Baker, 1987), 92.

3. Constance Cumbey, *Hidden Dangers of the Rainbow,* revised edition (Shreveport: Huntington House Publishers, 1983), 50. See also 46 and 122.

4. Ibid., 46. See also 113.

5. Ibid., 50.

6. Ibid., 122.

7. Ibid., 34.

8. Ibid., 50. See also 114.

9. See, for example, Dave Hunt and T. H. McMahon, *The Seduction of Christianity* (Eugene: Harvest House, 1985), 85. We even held a similar erroneous view of Genesis 3:5 at one time. See our *Answers to the Cultist at Your Door* (Eugene: Harvest House, 1981), 147.

10. Ed Decker, "The Sure Sign of the Nail," *Saints Alive in Jesus Newsletter,* 1987.

11. Personal interview, January 1988.

12. Texe Marrs, *Dark Secrets of the New Age* (Wheaton: Crossway Books, 1987), 250 (italics added for emphasis).

13. *Christianity Today,* 3 September 1983, 56.

14. Danny Korem, *The Fakers* (Grand Rapids: Baker, 1980), 46.

Chapter 6 You Could Be Next

1. Dave Hunt and T. H. McMahon, *The Seduction of Christianity* (Eugene: Harvest House, 1985), 192.

2. Ibid., 193.

3. Dave Hunt, *Christian Information Bureau Bulletin* (July 1986), 1.

4. Dave Hunt, *Christian Information Bureau Bulletin* (September 1986), 1.

5. Or see John Carter and Richard Moline, "The Nature and Scope of Integration: A Proposal," *Journal of Psychology and Theology,* 4:1 (1976), 2–14.

6. A contemporary manifestation of classic postmillennialism discussed in Chapter 8.

7. Constance Cumbey, *Hidden Dangers of the Rainbow,* revised edition (Shreveport: Huntington House Publishers, 1983), 152–153.

8. F. V. Scott, "John Wimber and the Vineyard Ministries," *Passport* (January-February 1988), 18–22.

9. Ibid., 20.

10. Bob Passantino, *Cornerstone* 15:78.

11. Dave Hunt, *Cornerstone* 15:79.

12. Mary Stewart Relfe, *When Your Money Fails* (Montgomery: Ministries, Inc., 1981).

13. Mary Stewart Relfe, *The New Money System* (Montgomery: Ministries, Inc., 1982).

14. F. LaGard Smith, *Out on a Broken Limb* (Eugene: Harvest House, 1986), 201.

Chapter 7 People They're Slandering

1. Each of us, no matter how noble our calling or how mature our walk, can be criticized fairly for our shortcomings. Each of the individuals and groups we discuss in the next three chapters can and have been criticized fairly on particular fail-

ings. But this book is concerned with *witch hunting* criticisms, not legitimate criticisms.

2. *The Los Angeles Times* (3 January 1987).

3. Dave Hunt, *Christian Information Bureau Bulletin* (July 1986), 1.

4. Dave Hunt, *Christian Information Bureau Bulletin* (September 1986), 1.

5. See Dave Hunt, *Beyond Seduction* (Eugene: Harvest House, 1987), 170, where he says Dobson "is devoted to serving the Lord and . . . has been used of God for much good."

6. Letter, 26 September 1987.

7. James Dobson, *The Strong-Willed Child* (Wheaton: Tyndale, 1987), 234–235.

8. *Psycho-Heresy* (Santa Barbara: Eastgate Publishers, 1987), 58–59.

9. Hunt and T. H. McMahon, *The Seduction of Christianity*, 192–193.

10. Hunt, *Beyond Seduction*, 169–172.

11. John D. Carter, "Secular and Sacred Models of Psychology and Religion," *Journal of Psychology and Theology* 5:30 (1977), 202.

12. James Dobson, *Preparing for Adolescence* (Ventura: Vision House [Regal], 1978), 31–32.

13. James Dobson, "The Plan of Salvation," broadcast on "Focus on the Family" (Pomona: Focus on the Family, 18 September 1987, [emphasis ours]).

14. Ibid.

15. Tim Brown, *Prevue* (Seattle: Colossian Fellowship, September 1985), 24–25.

16. Hunt and T. H., *The Seduction of Christianity*, 82–84.

17. Brown, *Prevue* (June 1985), 25.

18. Hunt and McMahon, *Seduction*, 83.

19. Casey Treat, "Believing in Yourself" (September 1983), and also quoted in *Seduction*, 82–83.

20. Tim Brown letter to Dave Hunt, 15 May 1985.

21. Dave Hunt letter to Tim Brown, 17 May 1985.

22. Dave Hunt letter to Tim Brown, 13 September 1985.

23. Brown, *Prevue* (June 1985), 11–12.

24. Ibid.

25. Our purpose in this book does not include lengthy examina-

tions of the teachings of those accused by witch hunting techniques. See "For Further Reading" for books which refute Treat's position.

26. Casey Treat, partial transcript of 12 June 1985 meeting with Dave Hunt and the Colossian Fellowship.

27. Tim Brown letter to Harvest House Publishers, 1 July 1985.

28. Dave Hunt, *Whatever Happened to Heaven?* (Eugene: Harvest House, 1988).

29. Tim Brown conversation with authors.

Chapter 8 Groups They're Damaging

1. Check with the Better Business Bureau for the town in which the organization is located; ask for a copy of the organization's most recent financial statement; do not support any organization if it cannot show evidence that at least 80 percent of your donation will go to the purpose designated.

2. Constance Cumbey, *Hidden Dangers of the Rainbow* (Shreveport: Huntington House Publishers, 1983), 161–162.

3. Constance Cumbey letter to Bread for the World, 3 September 1983.

4. Paola Scommegna (staff associate, Bread for the World) letter to Constance Cumbey, 20 July 1983.

5. We could make a good argument for reserving Christian terminology and labels for what truly represents biblical Christianity, but that is an entirely different issue from New Ageism.

6. There may exist evidence which, presented fairly, could legitimately criticize any group or individual targeted by witch hunting. However, witch hunting is never legitimate, even if its target might sometimes actually promote heresy.

7. *Christian Information Bureau Bulletin.*

8. Dave Hunt, *Christian Information Bureau Bulletin* (February 1987), 1.

9. Dave Hunt, *Whatever Happened to Heaven?* (Eugene: Harvest House, 1988), 43.

10. Ibid., 209.

11. Ibid., 221.

12. Ibid., 238.

13. Ibid., 283.

14. Georgie Kinyon letter to Cal Beisner, 5 October 1987.

15. Ibid.

16. Pauline MacPherson, *Coalition on Revival: What Is It?* (Denver: Bold Truth Press, 1987).

17. Ibid.

18. Despite having a relative involved with COR, we are still capable of objective evaluation of the charges against it. Biblical discernment looks at the evidence. Witch hunting dismisses it because of its suspect source.

19. Cal Beisner letter to Georgie Kinyon, 4 September 1986.

20. Ibid., 16.

21. For a good presentation of the arguments for and against Christian activism, listen to the debate "Is There a Biblical Basis for Christian Social Activism?" between Dave Hunt and Dr. H. Wayne House (Dallas Theological Seminary), sponsored by Answers In Action and Simon Greenleaf School of Law Debate Society. (Available from Answers In Action, P.O. Box 2067, Costa Mesa, Calif. 92628.)

22. Hunt, *Whatever Happened*, 208.

23. Ibid.

24. Ibid., 283.

25. Beisner letter, 8.

26. See "For Further Reading" for books which deal with this aberration within Christian groups.

27. *The Christian World View of Pastoral Renewal* (Mountain View, Calif.: Coalition on Revival, 1986), 4–5.

28. Gary DeMar, *The Reduction of Christianity* (Fort Worth: Dominion Press, 1988), 201.

29. There are variations within postmillennialism, just as there are variations within dispensationalism. Hodge, Warfield, and Machen differed in some secondary respects from today's postmillennialists, just as Lindsey and other dispensationalists differ in some secondary respects from Darby, Scofield, and even more recently, Ryrie and Chafer.

30. Criticism of reconstructionism from an exegetical perspective, honest difference of opinion, and well-researched, persuasive argumentation is not witch hunting and consequently is not dealt with here. The quotes from Lindsey, Cumbey, *et. al.*, are representative of the authors' *witch hunting* against reconstructionism, not of any *responsible* criticism they or others could raise about reconstructionism or any other orthodox eschatological position.

31. Hal Lindsey, *The Road to Holocaust* (New York: Bantam Books, 1989).

32. Ray Nelson, "Whose Kingdom Come. . . ?" *Passport* (January-February 1988), 3–5.

33. Constance Cumbey on the Lou Davies' Show, KPDQ Radio, Portland, OR.

34. Also Dave Hunt, *Beyond Seduction* (Eugene: Harvest House, 1987) and Dave Hunt, *Christian Information Bureau Bulletin* (February 1987).

35. The terms *reconstructionist, dominionist, dominion theologist*, and "Kingdom Now" advocate are all used fairly indiscriminately by critics. When we use the term *reconstructionist*, we refer to a contemporary activist postmillennialist. The other terms usually refer to premillennial activists who are primarily charismatics. For simplicity, the rest of this chapter uses *reconstructionist* most of the time, unless even the critic makes a distinction. There simply is not enough space to discuss the unscholarly mixing of all these terms and comparing the reconstructionists with all the beliefs and practices of the similar-sounding movements.

36. Lindsey, *Road to Holocaust*, back cover.

37. Ibid., 29–30.

38. Ibid., 98.

39. Ibid., 194.

40. Ibid., 196.

41. Ibid., 232.

42. Lindsey's qualifying statement, "comes dangerously close," does not really temper his criticism. Being dangerously close to spiritual fornication is like being almost sexually active.

43. Ray Nelson, 3–5.

44. Constance Cumbey, radio interview on the Lou Davies' Show, KPDQ, Portland, OR.

45. Hunt barely mentioned it in *Beyond Seduction* although we are told that his publisher cut most of what he wanted to say about reconstructionism out of that book.

46. Hunt, *Beyond Seduction*, 255.

47. Dave Hunt, *Christian Information Bureau Bulletin* (February 1987), 1.

48. Hunt and most other critics fail to distinguish between reconstructionism, dominionism, "Kingdom Now," or between reformed and charismatic theologies. We are using the one term *reconstructionism* for simplicity.

49. Hunt, *Whatever Happened*, 199.

50. Ibid., 212.

51. Ibid., 218.

52. Ibid., 230.

53. Ibid., 236.

54. Ibid., 276.

55. See "For Further Reading."

56. J. Gordon Melton, *The Hidden Dangers of the Rainbow: A Christian Response* (Santa Barbara: Institute for the Study of Religion in America, 1985), 2.

57. Gary DeMar and Peter J. Leithart, *The Legacy of Hatred Continues: A Response to Hal Lindsey's The Road to Holocaust* (Tyler, Tex.: Institute for Christian Economics, 1989).

58. It is interesting to note that classic dispensational authority C. I. Scofield did believe that saints in the Old Testament were *saved* by keeping the Law: "The point of testing is no longer legal obedience as the condition of salvation, but acceptance or rejection of Christ. . . ." (*The Scofield Reference Bible*, 1115, note 2.) Later dispensationalists omitted this sentence from the revised version of this Bible, *The New Scofield Reference Bible*.

59. Cumbey, *Hidden Dangers*, 154–155.

60. Constance Cumbey, *A Planned Deception* (East Detroit: Pointe Publishers, Inc., 1985), 119–122.

61. *Planned Deception*.

62. Ted Engstrom letter to an inquirer, 30 March 1983.

63. Ted Engstrom letter to Pat Robertson, 30 March 1983.

64. World Vision interoffice memo, 21 March 1983.

65. *World Vision Annual Report* (1986), 9.

Chapter 9 Counter-Cult Ministries They're Attacking

1. *Cornerstone*'s parent organization, Jesus People USA, also ministers in many other areas besides cults.

2. We prepared this summary from a talk Cumbey gave at a Houston prophecy conference held 13–14 November 1987.

3. Brooks Alexander, interview with authors, March, 1988.

4. Bantam Books, Lindsey's publisher, actually has an entire line of New Age books. We realize that reconstructionist Gary North used almost this same line about Lindsey's book in one of his newsletters. North was being facetious. Cumbey is serious.

5. Karen Hoyt and the Spiritual Counterfeits Project, *The New Age Rage* (Old Tappan, N.J.: Revell, 1987), 12.

6. Ibid.

7. Ibid.

8. SCP cannot be under the condemnation of guilt by association since neither they nor Karen Hoyt were even invited to or present at the conference.

9. See note 2, this chapter.

10. Alice Bailey is the writer Cumbey repeatedly identifies as the human master planner of the New Age Movement.

11. Constance Cumbey, summarized from a radio interview on KTED, Fowler, Calif., 5 June 1983.

12. Eric Pement letter to Dave Hunt, 11 October 1983, 7–8.

13. Constance Cumbey, *A Planned Deception* (East Detroit: Pointe Publishers, Inc., 1985), 16.

14. Ibid., 70.

15. Constance Cumbey radio interview, Lou Davies' Show, KPDQ, Portland, OR.

16. Walter Martin, October 1983.

17. The entire paper is available by writing CRI, P.O. Box 500, San Juan Capistrano, Calif. 92693.

18. Elliot Miller, *A Reply to Constance Cumbey's Charges Against Walter Martin and CRI* (San Juan Capistrano: CRI, 1988), 2–3.

19. Ibid., 4–5.

20. Ibid.

21. Ibid., 10.

For Further Reading

Anonymous. *Eerdman's Handbook to Christianity in America.* Grand Rapids, MI: William B. Eerdmans Publishing Company, 1983.

Barron, Bruce. *The Health and Wealth Gospels.* Downers Grove, IL: InterVarsity Press, 1987.

Barrs, Jerram. *Shepherds and Sheep.* Downers Grove, IL: InterVarsity Press, 1983.

Berkhof, L. *The History of Christian Doctrines.* Grand Rapids, MI: Baker Book House, 1937.

Bettenson, Henry, ed. *Documents of the Early Church.* New York: Oxford University Press, 1963 (second edition).

Bloesch, Donald. *Faith and Its Counterfeits.* Downers Grove, IL: InterVarsity Press, 1981.

Bobgan, Martin and Deidre. *Psycho-Heresy.* Santa Barbara, CA: Eastgate Publishers, 1987.

Bouman, Herbert J. *A Look at Today's Churches—A Comparative Guide.* St. Louis, MO: Concordia Publishing House, 1980.

Bray, Gerald. *Creeds, Councils, and Christ.* Downers Grove, IL: InterVarsity Press, 1984.

Brown, Harold O. J. *Heresies.* Garden City, NJ: Doubleday & Company, 1984.

Browning, Don S. *Religious Thought and the Modern Psychologies.* Philadelphia, PA: Fortress Press, 1987.

Bule, Florence. *"God Wants You Rich" and Other Enticing Doctrines*. Minneapolis, MN: Bethany House Publishers, 1983.

Buswell, James Oliver. *A Systematic Theology of the Christian Religion*. Grand Rapids, MI: Zondervan Publishing House, 1962.

Carson, D. A. *Exegetical Fallacies*. Grand Rapids, MI: Baker Book House, 1984.

Cohn, Norman. *The Pursuit of the Millennium*. New York: Oxford University Press, 1961, 1970.

Collins, Gary. *Can You Trust Psychology?* Downers Grove, IL: InterVarsity Press, 1988.

Coniaris, Anthony M. *Introducing the Orthodox Church: Its Faith and Life*. Minneapolis, MN: Light and Life Publishing Company, 1982.

Cumbey, Constance. *The Hidden Dangers of the Rainbow*. Shreveport, LA: Huntington House, Inc., 1983 (revised edition).

_____. *A Planned Deception*. East Detroit, MI: Pointe Publishers, Inc., 1985.

DeMar, Gary and Peter Leithart. *The Legacy of Hatred Continues: A Response to Hal Lindsey's The Road to Holocaust*. Tyler, TX: Institute for Christian Economics, 1989.

_____. *The Reduction of Christianity*. Ft. Worth, TX: Dominion Press, 1988.

Dobson, James. *The Strong-Willed Child*. Wheaton: IL: Tyndale Publishers, 1978.

_____. *Preparing for Adolescence*. Ventura, CA: Regal Books/Vision House, 1987.

Downing, David. *What You Know Might Not Be So*. Grand Rapids, MI: Baker Book House, 1987.

Eidsmoe, John. *Christianity and the Constitution*. Grand Rapids, MI: Baker Book House, 1987.

Elwell, Walter A., ed. *Evangelical Dictionary of Theology*. Grand Rapids, MI: Baker Book House, 1984.

Erickson, Millard J. *Contemporary Options in Eschatology*. Grand Rapids, MI: Baker Book House, 1977.

Ferguson, Sinclair B., David F. Wright and J. I. Packer. *New Dictionary of Theology:* Downers Grove, IL: InterVarsity Press, 1988.

Feynman, Richard. *Surely You're Joking Mr. Feynman*. New York: W. W. Norton and Company, 1985.

Geisler, Norman. *Ethics: Alternatives and Issues*. Grand Rapids, MI: Zondervan Publishing House, 1971.

_____. *False Gods of Our Time*. Eugene, OR: Harvest House Publishers, 1985.

_____ and William D. Watkins. *Worlds Apart*. Grand Rapids, MI: Baker Book House, 1989.

Groothuis, Douglas. *Unmasking the New Age*. Downers Grove, IL: InterVarsity Press, 1986.

Guthrie, Donald. *New Testament Theology*. Downers Grove, IL: InterVarsity Press, 1981.

Hackett, Stuart. *The Reconstruction of the Christian Revelation Claim*. Grand Rapids, MI: Baker Book House, 1984.

Harrison, Everett F., editor-in-chief. *Baker's Dictionary of Theology*. Grand Rapids, MI: Baker Book House, 1960.

Henry, Carl F. H., ed. *Basic Christian Doctrines*. New York: Holt, Rinehart and Winston, 1962.

_____. *Fundamentals of the Faith*. Grand Rapids, MI: Zondervan Publishing House, 1969.

Hodge, Charles. *Systematic Theology*. Grand Rapids, MI: William B. Eerdmans Publishing Company, 1973 reprint (3 volumes).

Hoekema, Anthony. *The Four Major Cults*. Grand Rapids, MI: William B. Eerdmans Publishing Company, 1963.

Hoyt, Karen and the Spiritual Counterfeits Project. *The New Age Rage*. Old Tappan, NJ: Fleming Revell, 1987.

Hunt, Dave. *Beyond Seduction*. Eugene, OR: Harvest House Publishers, 1987.

Hunt, Dave. *Whatever Happened to Heaven?* Eugene, OR: Harvest House Publishers, 1988.

_____, and T. H. McMahon. *The Seduction of Christianity*. Eugene, OR: Harvest House Publishers, 1987.

Kelly, J. N. D. *Early Christian Doctrines*. New York: Harper and Row, Publishers, 1987.

Klass, Philip J. *UFOs Explained*. New York: Random House, 1974.

Klotsche, E. H. *The History of Christian Doctrine*. Grand Rapids, MI: Baker Book House, 1979.

Kole, Andre. *Miracles or Magic?* Eugene, OR: Harvest House Publishers, 1984, 1987.

Korem, Danny and Paul Meier. *The Fakers*. Grand Rapids, MI: Baker Book House, 1980.

Lewis, C. S. *Mere Christianity*. New York: Macmillan, 1974.

Lindsey, Hal. *The Road to Holocaust*. New York: Bantam Books, 1989.

Lohse, Bernard, translated by F. Ernest Stoeffler. *A Short History of Christian Doctrine*. Philadelphia, PA: Fortress Press, 1963.

Ludwigson, R. *A Survey of Bible Prophecy*. Grand Rapids, MI: Zondervan Publishing House, 1973.

Machen, J. Gresham. *The Virgin Birth of Christ*. Grand Rapids, MI: Baker Book House, 1930.

Marrs, Texe. *Dark Secrets of the New Age*. Westchester, IL: Crossway Books, 1987.

Martin, Walter. *The Kingdom of the Cults*. Minneapolis, MN: Bethany Book House, 1965, 1977, 1985.

————, gen. ed. *The New Cults*. Ventura, CA: Gospel Light Publications/Vision House, 1980.

Mickelsen, A. Berkeley and Alvera. *Understanding Scripture*. Ventura, CA: Regal Books, 1982.

Miller, Elliot. *A Crash Course on the New Age Movement*. Grand Rapids, MI: Baker Book House, 1989.

Montgomery, John W., ed. *Christianity for the Tough Minded*. Minneapolis, MN: Bethany Book House, 1973.

Moreland, J. P. *Scaling the Secular City*. Grand Rapids, MI: Baker Book House, 1987.

Parrinder, Geoffrey. *A Dictionary of Non-Christian Religions*. Philadelphia, PA: The Westminster Press, 1971.

Passantino, Robert and Gretchen. *Answers to the Cultist at Your Door*. Eugene, OR: Harvest House Publishers, 1981.

Payne, J. Barton. *Encyclopedia of Biblical Prophecy*. New York: Harpor & Row, Publishers, 1973.

Purtill, Richard. *Logic for Philosophers*. New York: Harper & Row, Publishers, 1971.

————. *Logical Thinking*. New York: Harper & Row, Publishers, 1972.

————. *Reason to Believe*. Grand Rapids, MI: William B. Eerdmans Publishing Company, 1974.

Ramm, Bernard. *Hermeneutics*. Grand Rapids, MI: Baker Book House, 1967.

Reiter, Richard, Paul D. Feinberg, Gleason L. Archer, and Douglas J. Moo. *The Rapture: Pre-, Mid-, or Post-Tribulational?* Grand Rapids, MI: Zondervan Publishing Company, 1984.

Relfe, Mary Stewart. *The New Money System*. Montgomery, AL: Ministries, Inc. 1982.

_____. *When Your Money Fails*. Montgomery, AL: Ministries, Inc., 1981.

Rubin, Ronald G. and Charles M. Young. *Logic Made Simple*. Claremont, CA: Arete Press, 1983.

Schaff, Philip. *The Creeds of Christendom*. Grand Rapids, MI: Baker Book House, 1877, 1919.

Smith, F. LaGard. *Out on a Broken Limb*. Eugene, OR: Harvest House Publishers, 1986.

Stevens, William Wilson. *Doctrines of the Christian Religion*. Grand Rapids, MI: William B. Eerdmans Publishing Company, 1967.

Tenney, Merrill C. *The Bible: The Living Word of Revelation*. Grand Rapids, MI: Zondervan Publishing House, 1968.

Terry, Milton S. *Biblical Hermeneutics*. Grand Rapids, MI: Zondervan Publishing House, 1974 ed.

Torrey, R. A. *What the Bible Teaches*. Old Tappan, NJ: Fleming H. Revell Company, 1933.

Tucker, Bruce. *Twisting the Truth*. Minneapolis, MN: Bethany House Publishers, 1987.

Walton, Robert G. *Chronological and Background Charts of Church History*. Grand Rapids, MI: Zondervan Publishing House, 1986.

WFF'N PROOF. *Propaganda* (game). Ann Arbor, MI: WFF'N PROOF, 1975.

Young, Warren C. *A Christian Approach to Philosophy*. Grand Rapids, MI: Baker Book House, 1954.

Youssef, Michael. *He-ism Versus Me-Ism*. Eugene, OR: Harvest House Publishers, 1987.

About the Authors

Bob and Gretchen Passantino are the directors of Answers in Action, a nonprofit educational organization. They have more than seventeen years of experience in Christian apologetics, and they have shared their expertise through personal evangelism, teaching, speaking, radio, television, and contributing to the research and writing of dozens of books on religion, the cults, theology, and apologetics. The late Dr. Walter Martin and his organization, The Christian Research Institute, frequently drew upon the Passantino's abilities in their apologetics activities. *Answers to the Cultist at Your Door*, authored by the Passantinos, has been set apart by reviewers since its publication in 1981 as a clear, practical, and authoritative discussion on the cults. It even received the Gold Medallion Award in Christian Education within a year of its release.

If you would like to draw on the experience of Bob and Gretchen Passantino, you may write them at:

ANSWERS IN ACTION
P.O. Box 2067
Costa Mesa, CA 92628